A Thousand and One

A Thousand and One

A Flight Engineer Leader's War from the
Thousand Bomber Raids to the Battle of Berlin

Flight Lieutenant Humphrey Phillips DFC MiD (twice)

with Sean Feast

An imprint of
MENTION THE WAR PUBLICATIONS

First published in the United Kingdom in 2017 by Bomber Command Books, an imprint of Mention the War Ltd. Leeds LS28 5HA, England.

Cover design: Topics – The Creative Partnership www.topicdesign.co.uk
Cover image: D.R. Knock, B.Sc. www.desknock.co.uk

A CIP catalogue reference for this book is available from the British Library

ISBN 978-1-911255-24-6

Contents

About the Authors

Humphrey Phillips was an apprentice car mechanic who volunteered for service in the Royal Air Force in 1940. He flew both the Halifax and Lancaster as an instructor and on operations, being awarded the Distinguished Flying Cross (DFC) for completing a tour of operations during the Battle of Berlin in 1943/44. He was twice Mentioned in Despatches, of which he is particularly proud. After the war, he pursued a successful career in transport and logistics, latterly with the 600 Group.

Sean Feast is an award-winning PR Director and journalist with more than 30 years' experience, working primarily across the defence and aerospace sectors. He has written extensively about Bomber Command and Pathfinder Force operations in the second world war, and is the author and co-author of 15 books including most recently *Down in the Drink* (Pen & Sword 2017) and *An Alien Sky* (Grub Street 2015). He was also part of the editorial team behind the Bomber Command Memorial book, *We Will Remember Them* (Fighting High 2012).

Flight Lieutenant Humphrey Phillips, DFC, twice MiD.

Chapter One – Town and Country

When I was born, my parents had been happily married for ten years and already had a daughter of five, my sister Eileen. My father had only recently been demobbed after four years in the Royal Army Service Corps and some onerous times driving a lorry behind the Western Front. My impression is that he spent more time driving away from the Germans than he did in supplying our troops on 'the line'. He was certainly no coward, but inclined to take heed of those who warned him on a regular basis to 'get out of here pronto!'

I come from a family of middle class European Jews who came to this country (at least on my father's side) in around 1780. My mother, whose maiden name was Marcus, has a more obscure lineage. Her origin was probably Russian and it is likely that only her parent's generation were British born. In my father's family, my grandfather (Humphrey James Phillips) was a well-respected secretary of a fashionable West End Jewish Synagogue congregation.

My early life was not an easy one, and I was prone to sickness. Not long after I was born (on 20 August 1920), a maid returning to our house was heard to remark upon seeing me 'Cor is 'ee still alive?' which suggests that my survival as a baby had, for a period at least, been in some doubt. At the age of five I had a swollen gland on my neck that our doctor decreed had to be removed. Coincidentally, my mother wanted my adenoids and tonsils removed, a fashionable trend at the time. She discovered that the services of a surgeon of good repute were available at a children's nursing home in Broadstairs. I was duly installed there and soon after found myself under the knife.

About half an hour after the operation the Ward Sister looked at me and asked me if I was alright. She was concerned at my bright red cheeks and decided that the neck bandage was throttling me! I was aware of the unusual way it had been applied by the Theatre Nurse, who had remarked to an assistant that she should pass the bandage under my arms and across my chest, because it would be more secure and keep the dressing in place. Alas, it was perhaps a little too secure.

On returning to London minus gland and tonsils, it was not long before our doctor was advising my parents to move me out of London (we were at the

Left: Humphrey's parents. Right: Young Humphrey as a schoolboy. His father did not approve of the time he spent studying the local wildlife.

time living in Kilburn) to a place with cleaner air. While this was being sorted, I started going to school, in my case the Maria Grey College in Brondesbury Park. My father, interrogating me during the first term, was far from satisfied with the curriculum. He did not approve of the time we spent in the local park studying the wildlife!

In the meantime, my mother had located the whereabouts of a nanny who had tended my cousins a year or so earlier. She had married a farmhand by the name of Ernie Mutimer living in rural Suffolk and was judged an ideal person to foster me, having only one adopted boy of my age. Thus, at the age of six I was sent away to Stoke Ash, a small village 17 miles from Ipswich on the road to Norwich.

The Mutimers lived in a four-roomed, semi-detached cottage in a dip that was surrounded, quite literally, by meadows. The unfenced lane leading off the main road reached the cottage in about a quarter of a mile. The village itself was about a mile up the road towards Ipswich; in the other direction, half a mile up the hill, was a farm.

I shared the back-bedroom with their adopted son, Richard, who had been a Barnardo's boy. The adults had the front room, into which protruded the staircase. The stairs started in the living room, the first two steps intruding in front of the door, sealing off the actual stairway. To complete the picture of such an austere property, the second ground floor room was the kitchen/scullery. This was almost as big as the living room, boasting the old-style kitchen range with an oven controlled by dampers, providing heat to the rest of the house. We did our washing and had our weekly baths in a galvanised tub that was kept in a shed outside.

Our water was primarily drawn from a deep well, 100 yards from the house. This fulfilled our drinking and cooking needs. For everything else we used the water that drained from the roof. Soft though this water undoubtedly was on the skin, I always found the dead insect life floating upon the surface a little off-putting!

When winter came, I learned just how tough these 'rural folk' could be compared to us 'townies'. The water used for washing and poured from an old-fashioned jug into an equally old-fashioned basin was almost freezing, the only plus side being that we tended to wash incredibly quickly.

Our living conditions were at best, primitive. The toilet was a hut at the bottom of the garden, and the Mutimers appeared not to see the need for any paper. They also didn't see the need for electricity; lighting was courtesy of the old-style paraffin lamps, and it was not until many years after I departed that the family installed a phone.

Our evenings were therefore short for there was insufficient light to read and no power for radio. Another reason why Richard and I went to bed early was the comfort factor: our seating in the living room was one of the two protruding stairs, with our backs to the door.

Despite our similarity in age, and our shared living conditions, Richard and I never became friends in the four years we were together. We did play games, but Richard had few if any toys and I brought none with me from London. There was little enjoyment. What I did develop a love for, however, was the rural scenery and always looked forward to our walks across what Ernie called the 'low meadows' extending from the cottage south east for some miles, with a footpath beside a stream and watercress beds, from which Ernie would pluck cress for our tea.

Another pleasurable memory was when I was bought a bicycle and learned to ride. Despite being a small, ladies model it was still too tall, and getting on and off proved a challenge. Close to the cottage was a large flat-topped stone which became my mounting step. Alas getting off became a problem, though I developed a technique for falling off without doing any damage to either me or the bike. This worked well until I experimented one day with a can of milk

When the weather improved, young patients were taken out on regular excursions.

from the farm at the top of the hill and spilled the lot. I was thereafter forbidden to use the bike for the daily milk run.

I had a strange encounter one morning while fetching the milk. A car stopped and a man alighted and came across the road to speak to me: 'Where are you going, sonny?' he asked. I explained, whereupon he added: 'Why aren't you at school?' Again, I explained, telling him that I didn't go to school, at which point he produced a notebook and started taking down details of my name and where I lived etc. He also discovered about my parents in London.

A few weeks later I learned that I was to be tutored by the local vicar for a couple of hours a week. My parents had broken the law by failing to ensure that I was being properly educated. My lessons comprised primarily English and Arithmetic, but I preferred it when the vicar's sons were down from university and I was entrusted to them. The curriculum was then broadened to include such useful talents as rabbit hunting with an air rifle!

In the time I spent at Stoke Ash, the pattern of life was influenced by two factors: firstly, I returned home for short breaks about three times a year, early autumn, Christmas, and Easter. The journey was achieved by coach and an incident on the first occasion has stayed in my mind. After my mother had picked me up from Victoria, and we had taken another bus to Kilburn, she repeatedly burst into laughter. Ultimately, I asked what was causing her merriment to be told that I had acquired a wonderful Suffolk accent. When

12

describing how Ernie's dog dealt with sheep, for example, I explained the use of 'ardles' to pen them which my mother interpreted as 'hurdles'.

These visits home were always pleasant and enjoyable. Primarily it was just good to be surrounded by everything I knew so well and to be able to play with toys that I didn't have in the country. As I grew older, from about eight onwards, I was able to add Meccano sets and trains as birthdays and Christmas presents. Despite my later leanings as a flight engineer, many of these sets and models were started but remained unfinished!

The other feature and pleasure of my 'holidays' at home was the chance to play with my cousin, Yvonne. She was two and a half years my junior and we got on well together and mostly played 'families' with one of her dolls which inevitably seemed to need the doctor to cure some imagined ailment.

Another memory clearly etched in my memory is my Sunday visits to see my mother's mother. My Grandma lived in a small, town house in Maida Vale, next door to Sir Edward Elgar, with my mother's two middle-aged brothers Harold and Jack. They looked after Grandma, Jack being the elder and rather formidable. He was later alleged to have made off with the family silver (although not literally) and disappeared to the Isle of Man. Harold was more pleasant and generous. Grandma, meanwhile, sat in an armchair and rarely spoke, other than to criticise the way that I ate my Sunday lunch. She was not much fun, and so those visits became more of a penance than a pleasure.

A more enjoyable aspect of being 'back home' was a chance to be involved with various Jewish festivals starting with Chanukah before Christmas (one to seven candles to be lit as the week advanced). At Easter, there was Passover which involved staying up late (always a good idea) and eating unleavened bread (which always seemed like a good idea until you're told to eat up and stop making interesting shapes with what is left). Strangely, I did not regret returning to Suffolk at the end of my 'holidays'; there was an inevitability to it that I simply accepted at the time.

Life took a sudden and unexpected turn in Stoke Ash when Nanny fell pregnant. For much of her pregnancy I was packed off home, and did not return until after the baby was born. She was a pretty child growing into a sweet girl with whom I became real friends. Sadly, she was only four, and I was 10, when it was decreed that I should leave the countryside and receive a more formal education.

My mother remembered that one of her old school friends, Sophy Goldhill, had a relative running a boarding school in Herne Bay on the Kent Coast. It was duly arranged for me to spend a couple of weeks there before the autumn term officially started. Among the other boys who was there at the time was Sophy's elder son John, with whom I became firm friends until his death in 2012.

Herne Bay was a sleepy Victorian seaside town and very different from the world I had known in the country. But so began three and half years catching up with the educational abilities of my fellow pupils (which I just about managed) and a chance to take part in sport and gymnastics which I both enjoyed. In the winter, we played soccer, and cricket in the summer. We bathed in the sea daily, regardless of the weather.

The school, Kent Coast College, had around 90 boys, and we were all housed in an old Victorian building with poor heating and rather feeble gas lighting. The classrooms, however, were cleverly grouped in one long hall, with a divider which, for assembly and other communal functions, could be folded back to create a single room.

This was a Jewish school, and as such all of the boys were coached for Bar Mitzvah at 13 which meant leading grace at table for every meal on the nominated day (which came around about once a month) and taking morning and evening prayers. We also had to assist with Shobus, the Saturday service recognising the 'day of rest'. These functions were good training for later life, not only to learn Hebrew, but also to speak to a large gathering, but at 13 we were ignorant of such merits and to me it was a slightly daunting bore. I'm sure others felt the same.

Learning the Torah was certainly a challenge. The Hebrew language characters as they appear in the scroll of the law have no vowels, and so you have to memorise sounds. This is all very well but you also have to chant those sounds to a tune. It took two or three months for me to be able to learn the passage that the headmaster had selected for me, and chant the whole 'Pasha'.

There was an even greater challenge, in that my Bar Mitzvah was to be held at the New West End Synagogue in Bayswater, under the auspices of the Minister, Ephraim Levine and the Chosen, Isaac Goldstein. The latter was responsible for my performance on the day and that meant being able to match his test of my religious knowledge and chant the Pasha to his satisfaction.

A further challenge was an invitation to visit the home of Elkan Adler[1], an influential congregant and brother of the then Chief Rabbi. He was a friend of my Grandfather and had somehow got wind of my forthcoming 'coming of age'. To me, visiting his rather lavish house in Bayswater, unescorted, was something of an ordeal, but he was kind and appreciative. My reward for singing a portion of my Pasha to him was a copy of one of his books (he was quite a distinguished writer in Jewish history) which I still have today.

On the day of the Bar Mitzvah itself, all went well, other than another misjudgement regarding my height. Being so short, I needed a stool to be able to see and read the Torah on the desk in front of me! Afterwards there was a celebratory meal at my home attended by the Minister, family and friends. A second party followed to which more friends were invited along with the Chosen. When I asked my mother why we had two celebrations, I was told that the Minister and the Chosen were not on speaking terms!

Beyond the obvious Jewish teachings, our education was similar to all other schools at the time insofar as the curriculum prepared us for passing the School Certificate and Metric. Even though I was 10, I had a fair way to catch up and was originally placed with the eight year olds. By the time I left, I had nearly reached parity with my peers but sadly my progress came to something of a halt at 13+.Sport and physical education was something I enjoyed and I was always up for some healthy competition. We had a gymnasium that was especially well equipped, with lengths of rope hanging from a large A-frame beneath the ceiling. On one occasion, John Goldhill[2] challenged me to a race, tempting me by saying that he had balanced a Fry's chocolate cream at the top of the frame, and if beat him to the top, I could have it. Needless to say, I did indeed beat him to it, but as I reached out to grab the wrapper, I discovered it was made of tin. It was a fake! I recall that I did not find it especially funny at the time and neither did our PE instructor, who later gave me a 'medal' at the end of the school term to recognise my effort.

---

[1] *Elkan Adler was an author, lawyer, historian and noted collector of Jewish books and manuscripts. He was a particular specialist in the history of the Persian Jews and travelled and wrote extensively on the subject. He died in London in 1946*

[2] *John Goldhill had an eventful war as a despatch rider, helping to manage and control traffic on D-Day, and fighting his way across Northern Europe until the end of hostilities. He died in 2016.*

Left: Friendship with an attractive nurse was bound to aid a young lad's recovery. Right: John Goldhill was a great lifelong friend of Humphrey, passing away in 2016.

On another day, I recall we were out in the large playing field and a group of boys were playing leap frog over a standing water tap. I was invited to join in and without a thought began to charge at the tap at what I considered to be a good pace to clear the hurdle. Unfortunately, being somewhat smaller than the other boys, I misjudged the height and landed dead centre, causing a scream of pain that I imagined could be heard in Margate. Matron was not entirely sympathetic, but had some form of lead ointment that she painted on the affected parts and after a couple of days the pain had subsided. Fortunately, as three daughters will attest, there was no lasting damage!

It was not long after, that slightly more serious medical issues began to trouble me. During the winter term of 1933, and with open chilblains on both hands, I acquired an infection, resulting in a swelling and deep abscess in the left armpit. Within a few days I was sent to a nursing home on the opposite side of

16

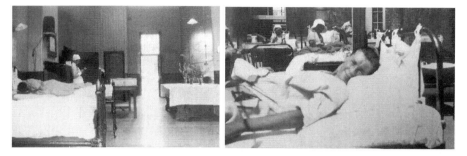

Left: The Lettsom ward was restricted to boys from the age of eight to 18. Right: In hospital, beds were moved outside on the veranda as part of the boys' treatment.

Herne Bay to our school. There I had an operation to lance the abscess. For about three months I remained a bed patient, through a painful period of drainage, before the wound would heal.

The plus side of being in the nursing home was that I fell in love for the first time with June. Sadly, she was a nurse in her 30s, but to me she was wonderful and our friendship flourished until I said something daft which clearly upset her and then had to endure several days of awkward silence. Happily, we resumed normal relations in due course and parted on good terms. One of the many interesting conversations we had was around religion, and she was obviously a devout Christian. We discussed the significance of various festivals etc. and I was thrilled one day to receive a visit by her vicar to explore the story of Esther in more detail.

Sleep at the nursing home was occasionally punctuated by sharp screams and shrieks which I worked out were associated with some of the patients giving birth. Whilst reproduction still remained something of a mystery to me, it was clear that the gooseberry bush story I had been happy to accept as a youngster was a hoax.

Meanwhile the doctor diagnosed that I had a TB infection, extending to the stomach glands, requiring specialist nursing. After the abscess had healed, I was thus sent to the Royal Sea Bathing Hospital at Margate to aid my recovery[3].

---

[3] *The Royal Sea Bathing Hospital had been built in the 1790s and founded for the scrofulous poor of London by Dr John Coakley Lettsom, a Quaker physician. It was a pioneer in the open-air treatment of patients suffering from tubercular complaints.*

17

The change of environment and routine was enormous. I was allocated to the Lettsom Ward which was restricted to boys from the ages of eight to 18. The 'indoor' wards were virtually unused; all of the beds, with the exception of those occupied by the most seriously ill (i.e. close to death) were outside of the wards on the veranda. They were equipped with shutters that were only to be used if raining or snowing heavily, and we had waterproof covers for the beds (again only to be used under the most extreme conditions). The secret of keeping warm in bed in those winter months was something we called our 'next to'. It was an extra blanket that we rolled around our bodies whilst lying between the sheet and was remarkably effective at retaining body heat. Sleeping under the stars in the summer, conversely, was a truly magical experience.

The routine was the same as most hospitals. I started as a full-time bed patient with close monitoring of my temperature and weight. Until the temperature was normal and my weight increased, I was confined to my bed. In due course, I was allowed to get up for short periods, to build my strength, and over time these periods were extended as my health recovered. After about eight months I was allowed out of bed for most of the day, and as the weather improved we were taken out for walks along the cliff tops or arranged the occasional game of cricket. We were supervised by the hospital porters.

Throughout my stay, teachers came in regularly to provide lessons in the morning and teach handiwork in the afternoon. Thus, I found myself adept at knitting, petit point and crochet!

By midsummer I was comparatively fit and anxious to return to a more normal life. My release coincided with the beginning of the school holidays and my parents came to Margate to spend the customary two weeks with me, living with Mr and Mrs Erridge, a couple resident in the town who boarded holiday guests. I was so content that my parents were happy to leave me with the Erridge family while they returned home. Mrs Erridge was pregnant and her husband and I became very friendly. He was a watchmaker and skilled stone setter and I spent many hours contentedly observing his work. I was almost tempted to tell my parents that I wanted to be a watchmaker too.

Mr Erridge was also a keen sailor and was building his own boat in the cellar of the house. I was invited to join him at the launch and all went well until we were a few miles from the shore and the engine stopped. The incident cooled my enthusiasm for sailing, and try as he may, Mr Erridge had great difficulty in getting the engine to restart. Many years later I tried my hand at dinghy sailing and found it much more appealing and considerably less noisy.

I returned to Kilburn as the autumn started and began thinking about a career. I was then 15. A Harley Street consultant, after examining me, suggested that when I reached 16 I should seek employment in an open-air environment, and if I wished to resume studies that I should do so at night school. There was talk of being apprenticed to a rose grower in Oxfordshire but I was less than enthusiastic. Ultimately, through the 'good offices' of our local greengrocer, I spent nine months with a market gardener in Horsepath, a small village near Oxford, living *en famille* with him, his wife, and child, a lad of six or seven.

Mr. Erridge was a keen sailor and fostered Humphrey's early interest in adventure.

The working plot was about three or four acres and he owned a horse and cart to transport his produce. He also kept a large and somewhat aggressive bull terrier outdoors in a kennel. To maintain supplies he also 'bought in' produce during the winter when Greens were especially scarce. I was free to do as I liked, but voluntarily worked alongside my host on occasion and went on his rounds to the poorer districts to the north of the city. Cutting the tops of Brussel Sprouts in the icy winter is not to be recommended, but I enjoyed handling the horse (a mare) and her willingness to work was a revelation. She was a wonderful animal.

I left Oxford in the early summer of 1936 and spent a very enjoyable time in Margate with the Erridges. My close family came to visit at different times and the weather was splendid. My father, in the meantime, had been talking to a

19

Left: Treatment included regular exercise. Right: Humphrey as a schoolboy. Carefree days where the key challenge was in learning the Torah.

business friend in St Albans and a garage was found for me to be apprenticed as a trainee motor mechanic. (My father had been a salesman for a silks and lining merchants, selling direct to tailors in every major town and city across the south east.) Until then I had shown no predisposition to engines or engineering, but shortly after my 16th birthday I started a new life living in digs and working in St Albans. I returned home (my parents had now moved to Willesden) every weekend, and in the evenings enrolled in night school to take English, Applied Mathematics and Machine Drawing. The object was to make good some of my educational deficiencies in line with my new career.

It was during one of my visits home that my father decided to add to my sex education, which thus far had been somewhat rudimentary. He knocked on my door while I was still enjoying a good night's sleep, came in and sat at the end of my bed which was most unusual. After establishing whether I had slept well, he cleared his throat (always the sign of a dramatic announcement) and said with rather more than usual emphasis: 'Son, I think it's time that you and I had a talk about sex.' With eager anticipation, I answered 'yes' whereupon he added: 'You do know all about it, don't you?' Feeling the excitement ebbing fast I responded rather feebly: 'Yes Dad, I do' and in a flash, he replied: 'That's good lad', at which point he got up and left!

My digs in St Albans were in a rather poor part of the city, opposite the Ballito Hosiery Mills in Hatfield Road[4]. After a few months, my parents helped me to move to better accommodation with the Wright family comprising a husband, wife and two children. Mr Wright was a professional printer and linotype operator, whose political views (as to be expected) were very left wing. I enjoyed many discussions with him, learning much valuable information about politics.

My new employer, Mr Carter, was former ship's engineer who owned a house on the Hatfield Road and a large garage opposite. It was a considerable plot comprising various lock-ups, workshops, and a sizeable covered building full of cars in various states of repair. My time at Carter's Garage went well, and I learned a great deal about the motor trade and how cars were serviced. I augmented this learning with further study of the subject, so that after three years I was quite a capable mechanic. I also learned how to drive and passed the test as soon as I was old enough, but while I was allowed to drive the cars involved in the business, my parents steadfastly refused to allow me near the family Austin 10!

While I had been mapping out my future career and transitioning to manhood, the country had been moving terribly and inexorably to war. I had little experience of what this meant, beyond an impression formed at school when some friends and I had sneaked away to watch *All Quiet on the Western Front*, strictly against our headmaster's wishes[5]. We were, at that time, in the period known as 'The Phoney War', and my parents had moved out of London to Chesham in Buckinghamshire. For a short while during the General Strike of 1926, my father had been a Special Constable (I well remember his truncheon, a long, vicious-looking stick, tapered at one end) and was therefore quite public spirited. This public spirit led him to volunteer himself and yours truly to take part in an exercise to test the response of our emergency services to a bombing attack on the town.

For the purpose of the test, we were to assume that Chesham had been targeted by German bombers, the cinema badly damaged, and there were dozens of injured patrons requiring treatment. My father and I were allocated as

---

[4] *The firm was taken over by Courtaulds in the 1960s and the factory is now the site of a large Morrisons.*
[5] *'All Quiet on the Western Front', based on the novel by Erich Maria Remarque, was made into a film in 1930 directed by Lewis Milestone.*

'victims', and reported dutifully at 10-00am on the Sunday morning for the exercise to begin. We were immediately despatched to the balcony as stretcher cases, and 'rescued' by the fire brigade who lowered us down, still strapped to our stretchers, feet first. Happily, they did not drop anyone. We were then taken out to the forecourt and laid on the ground beside a team of ambulances where we were assessed. The doctors then marked our foreheads with wax crayons to suggest that we had been given pain relief, and after a long wait in the warm sun we were finally loaded onto an ambulance.

The driver and co-driver of our particular ambulance were two very pleasant young ladies, with no clue as to the local hospital location. It therefore fell to me, supposedly now under the influence of morphine (the wax crayon had in fact melted from my head and was now illegible) to explain how to get there and direct them accordingly. The final straw came when, half way there, we got a puncture. And yes, it was me who changed the tyre. Though it may have been a valuable exercise to some, it was probably more valuable in exposing the inadequacies of our response to an emergency situation. I hoped that if and when the real bombing started, we had learned our lesson.

While Europe and the world held its breath in that early spring of 1940, my three-year apprenticeship came to an end and I was promoted to the rank of 'improver', a role I should undertake for a further two years but in my case lasted less than six months before the war caught up with me, or rather I caught up with it.

The blow fell in a rather unexpected way. Mrs Wright explained that she wanted to move her parents-in-law from Southend to St Albans, and needed my room. I knew that within a few months I was likely to be called up, but she was emphatic that she needed the room there and then so I took steps to expedite my departure. My father mentioned that the Royal Navy was recruiting skilled mechanics and that I should apply. On 1 June, I visited the local recruiting centre and was pleased to see that it was staffed by naval men and a medical team who seemed eager to wave us in. Within a few minutes of arriving I was parading around a 30-foot hut, stark naked, being prodded, probed and questioned by a small group of doctors, complete with pre-requisite white coats. I was also given an eye test at which point I noted a momentary hitch. The optician conducting the test looked hard at me and asked me outright whether I had learned his chart by heart. Somewhat indignantly I replied that I had not, but asked why he thought that I had. 'Are you a Hebrew?' he then said, somewhat unexpectedly. When I said that I was, it seemed to satisfy him that I wasn't cheating. And then the penny dropped: Hebrews read a chart from right to left! At the end of the test I was once again paraded, this time fully clothed, in front of the Petty Officer in charge of paperwork and administration. Although he was very pleasant about it, he told me bluntly I was no use to them as I was classified as C3 - medically unfit for military service. At that point, and as if to drive the message home, he tore up my papers and threw them in the bin!

I was now in something of a quandary. Mrs Wright needed me to leave, but my plan to join His Majesty's Forces had so far come to nought. I resolved to go back the next day and try again, but this time to see whether the Royal Air Force would take me instead. This time I would be rather less forthcoming about my medical history and hope that I would not be asked to explain the scar under my left arm. As it happened, the RAF seemed delighted to have me, and I was assessed as Grade 1. Despite returning to the same recruitment centre I had been only 24 hours earlier, no-one seemed to pay me much attention, including the man who took the eye tests who was the same gentlemen who was on duty the day before. The RAF flight sergeant handling my application informed me that I was to attend RAF Uxbridge barracks in two weeks' time (on 14 June) where I would be formally inducted and told when and where I was to report for duty. I duly complied and joined 149 other men for the ceremony to enrol into the Royal Air Force Volunteer Reserve (RAFVR), taking the King's Shilling. Then came the invitation that was to dramatically change my life, and set it off in a direction that I had hitherto not even considered.

We were drawn up in ranks, with approximately 50 men in each 'block', so that the flight sergeant could address us: "Listen carefully," he said, "and when I have finished you will have three minutes to make up your minds. At our technical training school at St Athan, which is in South Wales in case you didn't know, we have immediate vacancies for 50 men to train as flight mechanics. If any of you wish to accept that posting, you will remain here this morning and over the weekend be kitted out and entrain for St Athan on Monday. When I give the command 'three paces forward, move', those of you wishing to volunteer will step forward and the rest of you are dismissed."

Needless to say, on his command I stepped smartly forward and my future was sealed.

Chapter Two – Engines and Airframes

Having made my decision, I realised there was quite a bit to organise, and 'phone calls to be made. On the one hand, I knew that Mrs Wright would be pleased to have the room back for her family, but on the other, I had not yet had time to pack my belongings or clean up. My parents would have to do that job for me, complete with the apple cores that I'd left in the dressing table drawer. I also had to speak to my employer, and tell him, for the duration at least, he would have to do without my services as His Majesty had greater need. He was surprisingly relaxed and friendly about it, in direct contrast to his less-than-welcoming Staffordshire Bull Terrier[6].

On the Wednesday, a small party of us, including the newly attested aircraftman second class (AC2) H. B. Phillips 930313 (it was sometime before I made sense of the chap who told me I had an unlucky number), entrained for St Athan. On our arrival outside the No 2 Wing Headquarters, the unit flight sergeant almost had apoplexy when he saw our haphazard appearance and pathetic attempt to march and 'halt'. We had not yet been issued with our uniforms proper, and so no two men looked the same. He barked at us in the way that all senior NCOs were capable: "You rabble will be on the square on Monday morning and you will stay there until the end of the week," he told us. His normal intakes arrived having already completed six weeks of 'square bashing' on an ab initio course at Blackpool, and we were doubtless a tremendous disappointment to him.

So started our transition from civilian routines to a military life. Looking back on my six years' service in the RAF, two core aspects stand out: timekeeping and orderliness. The former is paramount, whatever your rank and regardless of who you are. Orderliness (and cleanliness) bear particularly hard on a lowly AC2 recruit, but thereafter and once learned, both attributes stay with you for the rest of your life.

I settled into my new home quite quickly, albeit that St Athan was a daunting place. It had been home to No 4 School of Technical Training since just before

---

[6] *Mr Carter wrote a reference for Humphrey that reads: 'To whom it may concern: the bearer of this, Humphrey Phillips, has been in my employ as an apprentice motor mechanic from October 1936 to present date on general motor repairs, mechanical and electrical. His only reason for leaving is that he wishes to join his Majesty's forces. He is a very good fitter and would become a very good motor mechanic and I am sorry to lose his services'. Mr Carter had underlined the word 'very'.*

the war and was divided into two camps, East and West. Across the site were permanent workshops, stores, and accommodation, and for leisure there was an amenity block with a church, gymnasium, swimming bath, and 1200 seat cinema. St Athan trained airframe and engine fitters, as well as mechanics, and included the first few members of the WAAF[7].

The course was absorbing, and I found my background as a motor mechanic to be most helpful. Curiously, perhaps, the corporal instructors (all of them regulars) tended to be less than enthusiastic or impressed with my existing skills, sometimes to the point of being contemptuous. Over the next twelve weeks, however, I made many friends, one opening my mind to some private study on aero engines and another encouraging me to buy his motorbike (a BSA 250cc).

At the end of the course we had covered the whole of the 'basic' syllabus including the rudiments (and detail) around the internal combustion engine, carburettors, magnetos, air-cooled engines, liquid-cooled engines, components, variable pitch propellers, aircraft servicing, and airfield procedures. Various engine types were available for instruction, including the Rolls Royce Kestrel and the Bristol Pegasus, as well as several American types which were then coming into service. The bulk of our time, however, was spent tinkering with the smaller four- and six-cylinder engines that were popular in the 1920s and 30s. Our experience of the larger engines was somewhat limited, a fact that nearly proved my undoing later in my career.

One morning we were on parade in our PT shorts and vests, around 150 of us standing in line, when the air raid sounded. Sure enough, the Luftwaffe appeared overhead and started dropping bombs at which point the NCO in charge shouted at us all to take cover. You therefore had the almost comical scene of dozens of white, fleshy shapes darting like rabbits under the nearest hut they could find!

I was both genuinely surprised and rather proud to have finished within the top six trainees (out of 150) in the final assessment. This resulted in being presented to the air commodore who led our passing out parade and a celebratory flight in a two-seater Miles Magister, a super little monoplane that was used as a basic trainer. This was a thrill and, being my first flight, a little scary. The aircraft had an open cockpit which meant donning a helmet, goggles

---

[7] *By September 1942, when all Fitter and Mechanic Training had finished, the Ministry of Defence (MoD) estimate that around 19,000 RAF and WAAF airframe and engine fitters and mechanics had been trained.*

The mainstay of Bomber Command in the early years of the war, Wellingtons were not the easiest aircraft to service for a novice Fitter. The aircraft above is Wellington PM-W, R1588 (Crown Copyright).

and flying suit for the first time. I was also kitted out with a parachute which added to my nervous state. As it was, I needn't have worried and thoroughly enjoyed the experience.

There were two further consequences of doing well on the flight mechanics course: I was promoted to leading aircraftman (LAC) and nominated for a further course to become a Fitter II E, the 'E' standing for 'engines'. A flight mechanic was considered a 'basic' trade, whereas a Fitter II E was a more exalted station. Indeed, along with our Fitter II A ('A' for airframe) colleagues, we were considered the most highly-skilled grades in the service. But before heading to Gloucester to begin my further training, I was posted to 103 Squadron to gain some 'hands-on' experience of working on engines.

The Squadron was based at RAF Newton to the east of Nottingham and had only been there a few months before I arrived. They had also only recently converted from Fairey Battles to the Vickers Wellington 1Cs, and upon arrival I reported for duty to the squadron flight sergeant in charge of aircraft maintenance (our beloved 'Chiefy')[8]. The Wellingtons were new to us all, as were the mighty air-cooled Bristol Hercules engines that powered them. It was not a type I had come across before. The Hercules was a 14-cylinder two row radial engine that was unusual because it was a single sleeve design with the

---

[8] *103 Squadron flew reconnaissance sorties during the early days of the war from bases in France, and was forced to retreat after the German invasion of the low countries in May 1940. By the time it returned to the UK, it had only a handful of aircraft still on its strength, and began re-equipping with the Wellington 1C from October 1940.*

purpose of providing optimum intake and gas exhaust flow to improve both its volumetric efficiency and minimise heat. At full bore the first Hercules engines generated 1,290 horsepower and the Hercules II was even more powerful (1,375 horsepower).

We were kept busy from the start and my two-weeks on the Squadron did not pass without incident. On one occasion, I was tasked with performing a 30-hour service on one of the engines which I dutifully completed. On the air test that followed, the engine 'coughed' on take-off, giving rise to something of a 'hoo-ha' about my Fitter credentials. I was closely interrogated by our Chiefy, but nothing further came of it other than I resolved that servicing aeroplanes was not going to be a long-term career. On reflection, it was perhaps surprising that I was given such responsibility with so little experience. It was highly skilled work; you had to be able to pull a petrol pump to pieces, for example, hone it if necessary, and then re-assemble it such that it still worked. It wasn't that I was out of my depth, but it was a lot to take in for a novice Fitter.

Two further events during my short stay at Newton are worth recording. The first concerns an edict on high that henceforward we were to protect our aircraft at dispersal points around the aerodrome at night from possible attack from German commandos. The fear of invasion or parachutists at that time was very real, and we were determined not to be caught napping. Thus, we were to provide one armed guard throughout the night at each dispersal. The practice became known as 'Sleeping in Aircraft Guard' and was mounted in parallel with the routine nightly guard duties.

The weapon we were given to thwart any such enemy infiltration was a Lee Enfield rifle and five rounds of ammunition. The problem was that my route to becoming a flight mechanic meant that I had somehow bypassed my arms training, and I didn't think it pertinent to mention it then. When it came to my turn to stand guard, I was driven out with rifle and pack to a cold and very windy dispersal, and with a cheery "have a good night" the driver disappeared into the gloom. I climbed into the 'Wimpey' and contemplated my situation, using my RAF-issue torch to illuminate the sumptuous appointment for a night's sleep. It was not only quite eerie in the machine but also very noisy because the wind was causing the protective sheet over the Perspex canopy to flap furiously against the side. Having resolved myself to the thought that it was just for one night, I began to settle down and relax, until I started to wonder what to do if the Germans actually arrived. Five rounds were not going to hold them off for long, but I thought I had better acquaint myself with the weapon nonetheless.

Sitting on the rest bed, I unslung my rifle and loaded a round into the chamber. I remembered reading something about 'pulling back the bolt' to get the round out and proceeded accordingly. As I released the bolt, the unspent cartridge shot out, whizzing past my left shoulder. Zooming across the fuselage, it hit the fabric covering the metal fuselage frame and, with a rattle, disappeared into the geodetics. What followed next was akin to looking for a needle in a haystack, but my persistence was based in the full knowledge that I would face a court martial if I could not account for the loss of one of my five rounds.

After what seemed an age of fumbling and stumbling around in the dark, attempting not to barge into anything important, I at last found the illusive bullet and decided to club any approaching German with my rifle butt, rather than experiment with trying to get a shot away. It was a very long night without a wink of sleep, and I was much relieved when the truck arrived at dawn and my vigil was at last over.

The second event worthy of note was a visit from a 'real' enemy, in the shape of an intruder who, without constraint, dropped a single bomb which landed in the first house in a row of married quarters in which I was billeted at number three. To be precise, the bomb, which failed to explode, landed in the garden of number one. The authorities decided that the bomb constituted a serious threat to personnel in the cookhouse which they promptly put out of bounds until the device could be defused by the bomb disposal experts the following week.

A field kitchen was duly established though the food was of dubious quality (compared to what we had been used to) and so we faced a miserable week ahead. As it was, our despair was short-lived. On Friday night, two of our number returned from a good time at one of the local hostelries we frequented, and decided to take matters into their own hands. They found a wheelbarrow and with considerable skill, care, and a great deal of luck managed to lift and move the bomb to a nearby meadow. The cookhouse was reinstated and our appetites assuaged. A few days later there was a loud bang when, unable to defuse the bomb, the disposal team had it destroyed in a controlled explosion.

Early in December, my posting to RAF Innsworth Lane for the Fitter IIE course finally came through and I was installed in what, on reflection, was

A typical group of young 'Halton Brats' larking around for the camera at Halton, where Humphrey qualified as a Fitter IIE.

probably the least comfortable and most unpleasant of all of my RAF experiences. The camp was miserable, the food terrible and the weather foul. In simple terms, the course was to convert us to an even higher skill level, and once again I did well, earning a further 'promotion' to instructor status, subject to completing an appropriate course at RAF Halton in Buckinghamshire where they trained Viscount Trenchard's famous 'Brats'. Happily, I did not have long to wait, and after five weeks at Innsworth I was posted to Halton for a further seven weeks training, at the end of which I returned to St Athan as a qualified Fitter IIE Instructor. I also had two stripes on my sleeve to denote that I had been elevated to the acting rank of corporal.

My new role was primarily focused on a section called 'Flight Routine' and centred around teaching new recruits about how to secure the aircraft and move them safely when on the ground. It also included starting the engines, and getting the aircraft airborne. This was doubtless all very worthy and necessary work, but the aircraft we used as training rigs tended to be ancient biplanes (such as the Hawker Hart and Fury) which were hopelessly obsolete. I taught trainees on how to swing a propeller to fire the engine (without taking your head off) and useful tricks like stuffing an airman's hat in the air intake to quell a carburettor fire. Whether such tricks of the trade would be useful to them on an operational squadron was a moot point.

In addition to my instructional duties, I also had to take my turn as corporal in charge of the station guard. The guards did four hours on and then two hours sleep, and alternated, but as corporal you got no rest at all.

It was not all work and no play, however. During that time, I managed to acquire a girlfriend in the Auxiliary Territorial Service (ATS), and whenever I secured a pass we would head off on my motorbike to Cardiff for some fun. Alas, I have not the vaguest idea of how or where we first met, and judging by my diary entries at the time, my relationship with Florence was both fraught and short-lived.

Events, however, were taking a turn. Among the friends I had made along the way were a number with an ambition to fly. Until then it had never particularly crossed my mind, and to this day I cannot recall precisely why I would want to exchange the comparative comfort and safety of St Athan for the terrors of flying at night over Germany. Six months after starting as an instructor I learned that the Air Ministry was looking for Fitters to become aircrew, in the new role of flight engineer.

With the advent of the first four-engined bombers, and a shift towards only having one rather than two pilots in the cockpit, a new category of aircrew was created in Bomber Command to replicate what our colleagues in Coastal Command had been doing for some time. The flight engineer was expected to look after such things as petrol supply cocks, boost regulators and engine coolers. He might also carry out certain temporary repairs to equipment damaged by enemy action, such as a broken oxygen lead. This 'jack of all trades' would also be trained as an air gunner, and replace the 'regular' air gunner in an emergency[9].

I filled out the necessary application forms and a week or so later (on 15 December, 1941) I was summoned for an aircrew medical. I passed this with only one minor query: the medico listening to my heart heard something that concerned him and sought a second opinion. The second doctor also appeared concerned and the two men went off briefly to consult. A moment or two later, however, they returned, having decided that my heart would probably last the war and passed me as fit.

---

[9] *The description of a flight engineer's duties is confirmed by Squadron Leader Marten of the Battle of Britain Memorial flight in communication with the authors.*

The organisation for training flight engineers in those early days was still rather ragged and ad hoc in character, and it was a full three months before I was at last posted to Dalcross, in Scotland, for my air gunnery course. Reaching Dalcross by train entailed something of an epic journey of some 17 hours, and one that was not improved by the fact that I had started to develop the symptoms of flu some 24-hours prior to departure. Before leaving I therefore had to obtain the signatures of what seemed like dozens of officers to give me a 'clearance chit' and secure what was termed 'the unexpired portion of the day's ration' which comprised a hunk of bread, a small piece of cheese, coco powder and sugar!

On arrival at No 2 Air Gunners School (2 AGS) Dalcross my condition had deteriorated. I was coughing, wheezing and short of breath and I was almost immediately incarcerated in the sick bay for six days, having been diagnosed with Bronchitis. It meant that I missed the start of my course (I was part of Course 16A) and most of the ground instruction, but the CO was both kind and practical, allowing me to catch up by having instruction on a one-to-one basis.

Although my first encounter with a loaded weapon in guarding a Wellington had not been especially auspicious, I found that I took to gunnery surprising well. The flying component of the course was undertaken in Bolton Paul Defiants, a turreted day fighter that had very quickly been found wanting when the real shooting started during the Battle of France, and had very speedily been relegated to a night fighting role. By the spring of 1942 it was also a mainstay in helping to train air gunners, and I took my first trip with Sergeant Willison on 16 March to fire off 100 rounds into the sea. I completed nine such flights with a variety of different pilots fulfilling a variety of different exercises and was airsick on every occasion. The venting of the Defiant left a great deal to be desired, and the turret always seemed to fill with noxious exhaust fumes not long after take-off. The only bright light in my otherwise gloomy existence was that the views of the Moray Firth were spectacular.

One of the specific techniques we were taught was 'relative speed sighting', crucial to which was a detailed knowledge of enemy aircraft – their length, wing span, speed etc. Armed with such knowledge we would set the sight according to statistics we had memorised and estimate the difference in speed between the enemy and ourselves by the time it took to cross the sight. From this we would estimate the amount of 'lead' required and then open fire. In reality, by the time you'd done all of this, the enemy would have shot you

Woefully vulnerable in the Battle of Britain as a fighter, the Boulton Paul Defiant was relegated to a new role, training air gunners. The turret always seemed to fill with noxious fumes.

down! One of my contemporaries, a Pole, had his own aiming technique: the Bolton Paul turret was controlled by a joystick; his answer was to place the enemy aircraft in the centre of his sight 'and stir!'

In a record time of 21 days (the course typically lasted eight weeks) I qualified with an exam pass of 78 percent and was certified as an air gunner, our chief instructor noting that I was a reliable type who 'would make a good gunner'. Having looked at my air-firing results, never achieving more than nine percent hits, I would have to take his word for it.

On 29 March, I was on the move again, this time reporting to 102 Squadron, part of 4 Group Bomber Command. The Squadron was based at RAF Topcliffe in Yorkshire, so for once I did not have so far to travel. Under the command of Wing Commander Sydney Bintley, the squadron had already attained a proud reputation and started the process of converting from its twin-engined Whitleys, which had been one of the mainstays of Bomber Command in the early war years, to the four-engined Halifax. My training continued, being split into two distinct 'streams': 'Engines' instruction was delivered in the station workshops; 'Airframes' via a manufacturer's course at English Electric in Preston[10].

The latter course was marked by two pieces of farce: Firstly, I was detailed to be in charge of 11 other airmen, and instructed to report to the police station in Preston for our billets. This I duly did and was given an address in a rather seedy part of the town and directed to a run-down Victorian terraced house over five floors. The landlady in this dismal property subjected us to a running commentary on every equally dismal room. It included detail of the fate of each previous occupant, all of whom seemed to have succumbed to some dreadful illness or other, such that I turned around to find half of my squad had disappeared to find digs elsewhere.

Those who remained took our rooms and began to unpack, but the following day a rumour reached me that a girl in the basement bedroom was very ill. That evening, the landlady informed me that the girl had Typhoid, and said she would leave me to take whatever action I deemed appropriate. I contacted the station sick quarters at RAF Broughton[11] who advised a collective visit the next day. We were thus given the necessary jabs, and aside from one of our number fainting at the sight of a needle, we none of us contracted the disease. The second piece of farce took place when we arrived at the factory to commence our training. We were met by the factory manager with news that the instructor was not due for another week, and he therefore had no idea what to do with us. I did my best to explain our needs but could judge from his reaction that my words were falling on deaf ears. We thus found ourselves each allocated to a different section of the factory and were set to work helping to produce parts for the mighty bomber, in my case bending hydraulic pipes.

The course at Preston lasted two weeks, our instructor finally arriving and treating us to a blow by blow account of some spectacular raid in which he'd recently been involved. We returned to Topcliffe in early May and I found myself permanently attached to 102 Squadron's Conversion Flight, helping to teach pilots and crews to convert from two engines to four. Little did I know it then but this was the start of almost two years I would spend as an instructor, and experience some of the demanding and frightening moments of my flying career. But first the new Commander-in-Chief of Bomber Command, 'Butch' Harris, had need of us. Indeed, quite a large number of us.

---

[10] *English Electric's Preston works produced more than 3,000 Hampden and Halifax bombers for Handley Page.*
[11] *Today the site of Hawarden Airport.*

Chapter Three – One Thousand and One

By May 1942, Bomber Command, with which I was now a serving member, had changed quite dramatically in the two and a half years of war. In the beginning, we lacked the numbers, the aircraft, and the training to do any real damage to the enemy, losing a good many pre-war regular crews with very little to show for it. Throughout the Battle of Britain, the targets had been the invasion barges and other collateral that could support the threat of the Germans making it across the Channel. Once the fear of invasion had subsided, the priorities changed, as did the Commander in Chief. Sir Charles Portal passed the baton to Sir Richard Peirse and a clear instruction to destroy enemy oil installations and starve the enemy of the fuel to wage war[12].

In the spring and early summer of 1941 there was another distraction, as Bomber Command was called upon first to deal with the U-Boat menace, and later to attack the German navy's Capital ships, the most famous of all being the Scharnhorst and Gneisenau. They met with only limited success, and it was perhaps something of a relief to return to more 'traditional' night-time bombing raids on the Ruhr Valley!

This was an unhappy time for the men of Bomber Command, and its leader in particular. While Peirse was building up his strength, and new aircraft types were coming on stream, he was not enjoying the success he was looking for. New squadrons were no sooner formed than they were sent away for duty elsewhere, and the Manchesters and Halifaxes that promised so much were meeting a host of technical problems. As such, the faithful Wellingtons, Hampdens and Whitleys continued to be pressed into service, even though their sell-by date had long-since passed. Inevitably, perhaps, losses began to mount, as the German night fighter force began to shine and deadly flak and searchlight belts were established to hound the bomber crews from the moment they crossed the enemy coast.

A famous report was commissioned and published that showed the results of our bombing were even worse than expected, with some bombs missing their target by 70 miles[13]. The whole future of Bomber Command hung in the

---

[12] *Portal was elevated to Chief of the Air Staff (CAS).*
[13] *The Butt Report makes sober reading. Butt was at the time in the War Cabinet Secretariat, an assistant to Lord Cherwell, the chief scientific advisor to Winston Churchill. Butt was given the task of analysing some 650 target photographs taken during night bombing operations on 48 nights between 2 June and 25 July 1941 relating to 100 separate raids on 28 different targets.*

balance, and its reputation was not enhanced by the ignominy of the 'Channel Dash' incident in which the mighty Scharnhorst and Gneisenau, along with the Prinz Eugen, sailed from Brest to Germany through the English Channel right under our very noses and we failed to stop them. Despite the largest number of bombers being put up in daylight thus far, most were unable to find the ships because of bad weather. A handful were more fortunate, but not a single one succeeded in registering any hits. While not being a disaster of Bomber Command's own making, it was an embarrassing incident for all those who took part, but by then Peirse had already been side-lined pending the appointment of a new C-in-C.

As the 'junior' service, the RAF, and Bomber Command in particular, had to fight for its share of investment in new resources, and was not always successful. It was also a convenient scapegoat when things went wrong. This all seemed to change with the arrival in February 1942 of Sir Arthur Harris, whose term in office also coincided with a change in Bomber Command's fortunes. While the numbers of aircraft from which he could draw had not advanced in 12 months, the types of aircraft at his disposal were improving, and now included the first of the Avro Lancasters. He also had 'Gee', an innovative navigation device that enabled navigators to fix their position with considerable accuracy. Casualties, however, were still unacceptably high, and Bomber Command needed to prove its worth if Harris was to retain the interest of its supporters, the most important being the Prime Minister himself.

Harris knew he had to do something spectacular, and so came up with an idea of delivering a series of 'one thousand bomber raids', recognising both the actual power of such a force but also its propaganda and PR value. But there was one obvious snag: where to find one thousand bombers when you only have 400 aircraft available for operations? The answer, of course, was to harness the men and the aircraft within the conversion units and operational training units, and mix operationally-experienced instructors with crews coming to the end of their training. Along with a number of aircraft loaned by

---

The results were appalling: of those aircraft recorded as attacking their target, only one in three got within five miles; for aircraft attacking the Ruhr, the proportion was one in ten. The moon made a difference: in a full moon, two out of five found their target; in the new moon it was only one in 15. German defences similarly had an impact: an increase in the intensity of flak, perhaps not surprisingly, reduced the number of aircraft getting to within five miles of their target in the ratio of three to two. The harsh fact of the matter was that the real damage being caused by Bomber Command fell far short of what was being reported. In some instances, bombers were missing their target by as much as 70 or 80 miles.

35

Coastal Command, the target figure was thus achieved, and the plan was set in motion.

While Harris was doing his planning, I was settling in to life with 102 Conversion Flight, and getting to know its officers and NCOs, many of whom were precisely the experienced men our C-in-C was looking for to support his attack. Our Officer Commanding, for example, Flight Lieutenant Peter Robinson, was a young regular from New Zealand who already had the faded ribbon of a Distinguished Flying Cross (DFC) underneath his 'wings' that I later learned he'd won in 1941 flying with 78 Squadron[14].

Robinson was a slight, good-looking man with dark, deep-set eyes who was obviously well educated, articulate and intelligent. Although he was a Kiwi he did not appear to have much of an accent, and he was a man of few words. He already had quite a bit of operational experience under his belt and always gave you confidence when he was flying.

Robinson's Chief Flying Instructor (CFI), Pilot Officer Wally Lashbrook DFM, was similarly experienced, though at the other end of the scale in terms of age, indeed so much so that we called him 'Daddy' despite only being a pilot officer[15]. Like Robinson, he had great authority in the air, and was always

---

[14] *Peter Bettley Robinson, from Auckland, had been granted a short service commission in April 1940 and rose rapidly through the ranks. He was posted in to command 102 Conversion Flight on 12 January 1942 from 35 Squadron. On leaving the Conversion Flight in the summer of 1942 he was appointed 'B' Flight Commander at 158 Squadron and shot down and killed on 10 September over Dusseldorf. He was still only 22 years of age. Interestingly, his DFC appears in the same issue of the London Gazette as a DFC for Leonard Cheshire (Later VC, DSO, DFC) and a DSO for Percy Pickard, who 'starred' in the famous propaganda film 'Target for Tonight'.*

[15] *Born in January 1913, and educated at Okehampton Grammar School, Wallace Lashbrook had entered the RAF in January 1929 as a Trenchard 'Brat' graduating from RAF Halton as an LAC and later being awarded the first Fitter's prize. He had been a contemporary of Lawrence of Arabia at RAF Station Mountbatten and in 1933 volunteered for services overseas, being assigned to 100 TE Squadron. Selected for pilot training in 1936, Wally spent three years as a ferry pilot, amassing more than 2,000 hours of flying time on a variety of different aircraft. At the beginning of the war he was posted to 51 Squadron at Dishforth to fly Whitleys, taking part in his first operation on September 9, 1940. He received the DFM upon completion of his tour, and after a posting to Malta (to take part in an airborne assault to destroy a freshwater aqueduct in southern Italy) he joined 35 Squadron until a serious motorcycle crash put him out of action for five months. He joined 102 Squadron from 28 Conversion Unit. Wally's war was certainly an eventful one. Returning to operations in 1943, his Halifax was shot down near the French/Belgian border but happily he survived and evaded capture. On his return to the UK he was awarded the DFC and a Mention in Despatches for his evasion, and became a test pilot at*

Left: P/O Wally Lashbrook. As Chief Flying Instructor, Lashbrook had great authority in the air. Right: P/O Harry Drummond DFM, one of the doyens of the instructing world.

very 'definite' in his instructions and decision making. He never left you in any doubt as to what was required, and that was important when those decisions and such decisiveness could mean the difference between life and death.

Completing the 'trio' was another future 'legend' within the instructing world, Pilot Officer Harry Drummond DFM. In keeping with his peers, Drummond was also quiet, but personable, and extremely competent in the air. I had no idea until 70 years later just how many adventures he had experienced before joining the Conversion Flight, or how he had been decorated for his part in the attack on the German battleship Scharnhorst at La Pallice in the summer of 1941. His aircraft had been engaged by more than 20 German fighters over the target, and his gunners shot down two before he was obliged to struggle home

---

the Central Flying School. Released from the RAF in 1946, he pursued a career in civil aviation before finally retiring. He died in June 2017, during the preparation of this book.

on three engines and eventually landed on two. Not surprisingly the Halifax was a write-off[16].

There were also a number of interesting characters on the ground, and perhaps none more so than the one-legged station flight sergeant in charge of the workshops. Rumour goes that he had lost his leg in a motorcycle accident, and it was unusual in those days for the RAF to retain your services with any form of disability. It was even more unusual, as I later discovered, that he abandoned his ground role to apply for aircrew training. A pre-war regular, he was extremely knowledgeable on his subject and set the flight engineers' examination that we were obliged to sit. The paper was divided into various sections: hydraulics; power unit; electrical systems; oxygen economiser system; fuel systems; and drills. There was also a 'general' section dealing with such matters as 'George', bombs, and extinguisher systems.

Although some of the questions in the three-hour paper were comparatively straightforward, such as describing all of the methods by which the undercarriage could be lowered, others required considerable feat of memory, such as knowing how many fuses there were in the bomb circuit, or remembering what the electric switch was for that was mounted on the starboard leg of the starboard undercarriage and linked to the mud scraper![17]

The Conversion Flight had come into being in January of 1942 at Dalton, a satellite to Topcliffe, with ground staff attached from 1652 Conversion Unit (1652CU). With the arrival of the first Halifax aircraft (Halifax L9565), the 'conversions' began, the honour of being the first to undergo four-engine conversion falling to Squadron Leader Griffiths and Flight Lieutenant Williams. The pattern to the training was simple: captains would receive dual instruction first and undertake a series of circuits and landings to get a proper 'feel' for the aircraft before being allowed to fly solo. They would later be expected to fly solo at night. There was also ground instruction to ensure they understood all about the Halifax' fuel, pneumatic, hydraulic and electrical systems.

---

[16] *La Pallice gave the Halifax one of its first true baptisms of fire. Attacking in daylight, on a peerless summer's day, they were badly mauled but managed to damage the mighty warship. Peirse, the C-in-C at the time, sent a congratulatory message that read: "A magnificent day's work executed with characteristics dash and courage which the world now knows is the tradition of Bomber Command."*
[17] *Humphrey still has a copy of the original examination paper. There were 30 questions in all.*

Those first few weeks of conversion were constantly interrupted by the unserviceability of the aircraft, which became a source of ongoing frustration. Inexperienced ground crews were partly to blame, as was the lack of available spares. Radiator leaks and oil cooler leaks were a particular nuisance. The weather also played its part in slowing the process, with training frequently being cancelled due to poor visibility or adverse weather conditions, including snow. Converting pilots from two engines to four was not yet at the seamless stage it would reach later in the war.

By the end of March, half of the captains had passed their conversion course and been deemed operational, while the remainder were still part-way through the system. By the end of the following month, all bar one had gone solo, and the serviceability of the aircraft at their disposal had improved – though only slightly.

By the time I joined in the beginning of May it was quite a slick operation in its own way. We had half a dozen or so Halifaxes on which to train new crews, and most had been fitted with dual control 'sets' that accelerated things considerably. As a flight engineer, my role was to fly every time a new skipper was being trained, to keep an eye on the systems, instruments, and engines and ensure nothing was amiss. It was not always as easy as it sounds and conversion flying was not without its dangers.

This was still comparatively early days for the Halifax and it had been plagued with technical difficulties, especially relating to its tail assembly which was never satisfactorily resolved until much later marks were designed and available. All three instructor pilots – Robinson, Lashbrook and Hammond – would fly regular air tests for new or repaired aircraft, or simply to increase their hours on 'type' to enhance their experience. On 11 May, Robinson came to grief and only just got away with it.

His Halifax (V9982) was on a training flight with two pupil pilots, both Canadians. He was demonstrating the art of flying on two engines on the port side with the other two starboard engines 'feathered'. This was achievable as long as the pilot used more power (for a minimum airspeed of 140mph) and kept the aircraft straight with the rudder trim. With weather conditions deteriorating and one of the pupils at the controls, Robbie attempted to return to four-engined flying but neither of the 'stopped' engines seemed to pick up and they lost temporary control. Happily, they managed to get the aircraft

39

down in a field, but only just, and two of the crew were slightly injured. The aircraft was struck off charge.

It was in this same aircraft (V9982) a few days earlier that I had taken my first flight in a Halifax, oddly enough as the rear gunner, and with Squadron Leader Robinson (as he had become) at the controls. My first flight as the engineer came on 6 May, after which I settled into a routine of flying with Robinson and the other two instructors with their pupils on a daily basis, and sometimes twice a day. On one of my first trips, with Pilot Officer Mee and Flying Officer Hamilton receiving instruction from 'Daddy', we were obliged to land at Dishforth with a fractured tail wheel. The next day, and with the same two pupils, we had to finish our exercise early due to the failure of the starboard hydraulic pump drive. Such was the unreliability of our aircraft[18].

After only three weeks at 102 Conversion Flight I found myself in my car (I had long-since swapped my motorbike for a 'gutless wonder', an old Austin 10 that had a maximum speed of 48 mph) with my flying gear and personal kit on the way to Marston Moor beside the village of Tockwith, about nine miles west of York. It was home to 1652 CU, a bigger affair that was created to convert whole crews and not just the pilots.

The reason for the attachment was not immediately apparent, but there were many, like me, who seemed to be unattached. In short order, however, I was assigned a pilot and crew, and my logbook records rather teasingly a series of air tests and air firing tests conducted between 26 May and 30 May in Halifax R9432. Then, it seems, we were ready to go.

I remember little of the briefing in the early evening of the 30th, or the events preceding it beyond drawing my parachute and ration pack for what promised to be a long flight. The target was Cologne, and my first operational flight would be an historic one, taking part in Operation Millennium, the first ever 1,000 bomber raid, our C-in-C's PR 'spectacular'. We knew that the city would be heavily defended: there was said to be more than five hundred light and heavy anti-aircraft guns and a belt of some 150 searchlights, and our track would take us near to a number of night fighter stations.

---

[18] *Pilot Officer Leo George Mee was a New Zealander, later killed in action on September 24, 1942 with 102 Squadron. Flying Officer Sidney Hamilton went on to win the DFC and survive the war.*

Left: Sgt Eric Hay, mid upper gunner in the Thousand Bomber Raid crew. Right: P/O Ken Allport, who joined Eric and Humphrey in Harry Drummond's scratch crew on Operation Millennium, went on to serve with distinction in Pathfinder Force.

The raid had originally been planned for the 26th, but the weather over Germany had kept us on the ground. Harris was obliged to abandon his first choice of target, Hamburg, in favour of Cologne. If he was lucky, when we all got back he hoped to send us off again while the going was good and before we all returned to our home units.

We took after shortly after midnight, the 'we' being me, the skipper Harry Drummond, and what I took to be a 'scratch' crew though it soon became clear that I was the odd man out as the others seemed to know each other[19]. Of course, we were flying at night but we knew that we were surrounded by aircraft strung out in a 'stream' several miles wide. Key to success was the sheer number of bombers taking part that would saturate the defences. That's what we'd been told and that's what we hoped[20].

---

[19] *The crew comprised: Harry Drummond, pilot; Pilot Officer Ken Allport, navigator; Sergeant Frederick Simkins, wireless operator; Sergeant Frederick Hay, mid upper gunner; Flight Sergeant Libere Boucher; and Humphrey Phillips, Flight Engineer. See Appendix 1.*
[20] *Martin Middlebrook in the Bomber Command War Diaries says that the raid comprised 602 Wellingtons, 131 Halifaxes, 88 Stirlings, 79 Hampdens, 73 Lancasters, 46 Manchesters, and 28 Whitleys – some 1,047 aircraft in all. There were also a further 49 Blenheims and seven Havocs conducting 'intruder' operations. 1652 Conversion Unit contributed 12 aircraft and crews.*

Our route out took us down to Suffolk, crossing the coast at Aldeburgh. Climbing out was difficult, thanks in no small part to the weather and the ever-constant threat of icing.

Once we were above the clouds, however, it was easier, and so we remained on top of a thick blanket that stretched all across the North Sea and central Holland. As we came within 100 miles or so of the target, the cloud began to thin and disperse, such that as we started our bombing run we could see the ground quite clearly below us. And then we could see the first explosions, both on the ground as our bombs hit home and in the sky as a flak shell exploded, or one of our aircraft was set ablaze.

For most of the flight I had been occupied with the engines and ensuring maximum fuel efficiency. Fuel consumption could vary enormously, burning off typically around 200 gallons an hour at a modest cruising speed. At 3,000rpm, and with maximum (12+) boost, that figure would more than double. I had felt comfortable and at home, although there was not a great deal of room to move about and it was incredibly noisy. You could reduce the noise and vibration by synchronising the four engines, but that took quite a bit of skill and experience.

The flight engineer had his own compartment, facing aft, behind the pilot and more importantly behind his armour plate. There was nothing to protect me, other than the thought that if we were attacked, it would likely be from behind, and the canon shells would have to hit other members of the crew and the interior before they got me. Now as I was over the target, I had a conscious thought about what the hell I was doing there! Only a few months before I'd had a job for life if I'd wanted it at St Athan, but for some reason I'd chosen to put my neck on the line. It was all rather surreal. (Indeed, I wasn't meant to be in military at all; I'd failed my original medical!) The rest of the crew were all going about their business and I felt a stranger in their midst.

Our target was to the northwest of the main railway station and the Cathedral. We had the northernmost of three aiming points, and were among the last to arrive. Having been under attack for more than an hour, the German defences were more than alive to our presence, and shortly after dropping our bombs, we were 'coned' – caught in the deadly beam of a searchlight.

Drummond instructed me to fire off the colours of the day, the colours given to us by our Intelligence Officer as a 'ruse de guerre' to suggest to the German defences that we were in fact a friendly aircraft. There were a good many German fighters about. I made my way aft to a point just behind the wireless operator's station to retrieve the Very pistol and cartridges, ready to fire. Before I did so, however, I had a second thought. The day before the operation I had been talking to a fellow engineer with considerable operational experience who had encouraged me to take a box of small empty bottles with me and leave them beside the flare chute. He said that if we were ever to be 'coned', I should throw the bottles down the chute and the whistling noise they made as they fell would have the German searchlight operators diving for cover. I decided to put his theory to the test, popping a number of bottles into the chute to fall away into the night sky. Within moments of doing so, the searchlight left us, and so I returned to the cockpit, feeling rather pleased with myself.

"Did you fire off the colours of the day?" Drummond asked me as I took my place beside him. "No," I replied, "I threw out the bottles." What followed can best be described as a 'pregnant silence' but nothing further was said, and we landed back at Marston without further incident after a trip of just over five hours. It took my total number of night flying hours on the Halifax to ten!

The following day we were stood down and told that we could go to the pub as long as we kept our mouths shut until 23.59 that evening. My parents had moved out of London to Leeds, and so I decided to go and see them. I drove to their house and spent the day with my mother (who was at the time working with the WVS) and my Aunt. As we walked through the city there was a newspaper billboard with a screaming headline that shouted: 'Cologne Bombed' or such like. My mother remarked upon it and I said "I know, I was there" but they clearly didn't believe me. I started to explain and then realised that I had said too much already. It was again another surreal moment and one that many bomber (and indeed fighter) crew experienced during the war. One minute you could be over Germany, with the enemy doing their utmost to kill you and your friends, and then hours later you could be strolling through a park drinking tea as though you didn't have a care in the world.

On returning to 1652 CU we quickly learned that we would be taking part in another 1,000 bomber raid, this time to Essen. We were once again in the same aircraft and there and back in four and half hours. This second trip, as the history books will tell you, was nowhere near as successful as the first in which we had done tremendous damage to the town and killed a large number of its people. Many crews failed to find the target as it seemed to be covered in a haze that was typical of the Ruhr Valley. Casualties were only slight and the destruction caused was minimal. We lost 31 of our number in total to add to the 41 that had failed to return from Cologne. Our Conversion Unit lost one aircraft in each raid[21].

The trip was memorable for me because of the flying skills of our pilot. As we left the target area, Drummond came on the intercom to say that he would be taking her down to the 'deck' and staying there until he reached the coast. With my heart rate already going ten to the dozen, it seemed to accelerate even further as I envisaged all of the high-tension cables, trees and other obstructions we might hit at zero feet. Drummond's flying, however, was something to behold, as we skimmed across the countryside at full throttle, watching the patchwork of fields speeding beneath us. After thirty minutes or so the navigator called to say that we were approaching the Dutch coast, and to watch out for flak ships that we had been warned about at briefing. They were anchored out to sea, close to the shore, and bristling with light calibre flak guns that could inflict terrible damage on unsuspecting low flying aircraft such as ourselves.

Drummond acknowledged the warning and almost in the same breath we were hit. There were a couple of loud bangs, even audible above the noise of the engines, and a perceptible shudder. No-one seemed unduly concerned and there was even the odd humorous comment over the intercom that set everyone laughing. As the new boy, I was conscious of, and very impressed by, the crew's almost nonchalant attitude towards danger. This was clearly nothing for me to worry about, although after we landed we found a shell hole in the tail plane that might easily have caused us to crash. Such are the fates.

Daddy Lashbrook came to collect us (in Halifax 9987) and we flew back to Dalton on the afternoon of the 3rd.

---

[21] *Flight Lieutenant Stanley Wright failed to return from the trip to Cologne; Pilot Officer Harry Williams was lost on the raid to Essen. Williams had only recently been awarded the DFM for a tour with 35 Squadron. Both pilots survived to become prisoners of war. It is interesting to note that Wright was operating with a total crew of only five; one of their number was killed, the rest taken prisoner.*

By now I was no longer a 'trainee' flight engineer. I had been 'blooded' and was fully employed on the instructor staff. But if I wanted a reminder of how dangerous instructing could be, then it came shortly after my return to 102.

It was one evening, and I was the duty engineer left with the trainee pilot for his first night solo. The instructor pilot, 'Daddy' Lashbrook, had climbed out of his seat and was in the warmth of the control tower to monitor our progress.

All went well until we made our approach to land. When the second pilot responded to the instruction 'undercarriage down', we had a red light to show that the starboard wheel was not down and locked. This in itself was not a tremendous problem, and if I recall there were half a dozen ways of dealing with a loss in pressure so we thus went through the various emergency routines to find a solution but the wheel remained obstinately stuck in the starboard nacelle. Needless to say, we abandoned the landing while I tried to think through the problem.

As we circled at 1,000ft, the pilot called the control tower and Lashbrook asked whether we had checked the up-locks. I was rather indignant at this as we never used them, but 'Daddy' was insistent and I decided to check nonetheless. Making my way aft I was rather surprised to find one of our staff wireless ops on the rest bed, making up his monthly minimum flying hours. The up-lock control emerges from the fuselage side at the foot of the bed, and on this particular aircraft it had been fitted with an extension bar to make it accessible if overload fuel tanks were fitted. Our 'intruder' had pulled the bar out on which to rest his feet! I gave him an unceremonious 'prod' and no sooner had he taken his feet away then I was able to push the bar to the 'unlocked' position and the green light blinked to tell us the undercarriage was down. It was another lessoned learned, one of never to 'assume' anything and to expect the unexpected!

As a conversion team, we pilots and flight engineers had something of a 'roving' role, being despatched to other squadrons and conversion flights in and around Yorkshire and Lincolnshire to 'train' the instructors and bring new pilots up to speed with the aircraft they would fly operationally. It was towards the end of June that Robinson and I jumped into his car with a couple of 'erks' for a trip south of the Humber to Elsham Wolds, the home of 103 Squadron. It had established its Conversion Flight in the middle of June with Acting Squadron Leader David Holford DFC in charge and Pilot Officer J W Potts as the second flying instructor. We arrived on attachment on 23rd with a brief to convert the instructor pilots until the second week of July. The next day a third flying instructor arrived, Warrant Officer Reginald Fulbrook, bringing the Flight up to full strength[22].

Although then only 21, David Holford was already an established legend in Bomber Command and something of a celebrity. Early in the war, as a teenager, he'd flown with Percy Pickard, famous as the 'star' in the propaganda film, *Target for Tonight*. He'd also taken part in the infamous 'Channel Dash' for which he was later recognised with the DSO. A slight, diminutive character with penetrating eyes, he had two tours under his belt and it showed. I would get to know him well over the next year or so when he followed us to Lindholme.

Group Captain Hugh Constantine (photo: Chris Ward)

As the resident (and experienced) flight engineer, I flew two and sometimes three times a day, the usual pattern of dual and solo trips, four engines and three, occasionally with a trainee engineer cluttering up the front of the aircraft. As well as Holford, Potts, and Fulbrook, I also had the slightly unnerving experience on 25th of being joined in the cockpit by the station commander of Elsham Wolds, Group Captain Constantine, a man who clearly still liked to 'get some in'[23].

Our fortnight at Elsham had no sooner started than it was over, and we once again crammed into Robinson's little car for yet another move, this time to 460 Conversion Flight at RAF Breighton. This was an unusual move for us as the Squadron was Australian, and part of the Royal Australian Air Force (RAAF). Like 103 Squadron, it was part of 1 Group, even though we were effectively 4 Group

---

[22] *Fulbrook was an Old Haltonian (19th Entry) who won the DFC with 103 Squadron. He was killed in a flying accident on 22 September, 1942.*

[23] *Hugh Constantine had joined the RAF as an officer cadet in 1926 and rose to become the Air Officer Commanding 5 Group. As OC Elsham Wolds he took part in the first of the 1,000 bomber raids. He survived the war and retired as Air Chief Marshal Sir Hugh Constantine.*

Instructor staff at 460 Conversion Flight. Willie Caldow is centre, with 'Shorty' Fahey on his left, and Alfred Duringer to his right.

men under a different command structure. Such niceties seemed to have been overlook in the face of expediency!

The Flight had been formed in early June to convert crews from the Wellington IVs to Halifax IIs under the command of Squadron Leader Eric Campling DFC. At first, its existence had been somewhat chaotic; although they had four Halifax aircraft on which to train, they had no instructors, and an order had been issued that no-one was to attempt to fly the aircraft without a qualified flight engineer on board.

In ones and twos, the Flight began building its strength: the arrival of Flying Officer John Purcivall DFC as an instructor coincided with our own and we immediately set to work. I did not care much for Campling; he had something of an officious air about him, like a school master, but his operational record was again second to none, and it did not take him long to get to grips with the Halifax[24].

---

[24] *Campling was awarded an immediate DFC with 142 Squadron for his part in the attack on the German warships Gneisenau, Scharnhorst and Prinz Eugen on 12 February 1942. The*

In this widely-circulated photo of 626 and 12 Sqn Lancasters and crews at RAF Wickenby, Humphrey is in the group of five officers slightly to the rear of the crews in flying kit. He is second from left.

This was the first of four stints with the Australians, punctuated with a return to Elsham. On our second visit to Breighton, the Conversion Flight was now fully staffed and included three instructors with whom I was to spend the next 12 months and form a close bond.

---

citation reads as follows: 'After crossing the coast the aircraft accompanying Flight Lieutenant Campling returned to base with a defective turret, but using cloud cover Campling proceeded to the target area alone. He successfully delivered an attack on the Scharnhorst from a height of 700 feet, having dived from 1200 feet. During the attack, severe damage from flak was sustained to the port wing, elevator trimming tabs and the fuselage near the tail plane, causing control temporarily to be lost and the aircraft dived towards the sea. At 300 feet, before control had been fully regained, the aircraft was attacked by two Me. 109s. The Rear Gunner was unable to retaliate due to damaged hydraulics and only by the greatest piloting skill was Flight Lieutenant Campling able to evade the fighters and keep the aircraft out of the sea. By flying low over the water the pilot prevented further interception and by first class airmanship brought the aircraft to its base where he affected a normal landing with his crew intact and uninjured. Flight Lieutenant Campling has always shown a magnificent offensive spirit and by his own knowledge, skill and zeal maintains a high morale in his own crew and is an inspiring influence to all crews in the Squadron. His conduct cited above is held in great esteem by me and by his fellow pilots.'

The first of this trio, and the first to arrive at Breighton, was Flight Sergeant Francis Fahey, known universally as 'Shorty' because of his stature. 'Shorty' was by nationality, British, but in every other respect an Australian. He was married, and a fair bit older than the rest of us and more 'worldy'. He also had a three-year old daughter, Margaret. Interestingly, he'd been a gold miner before the war but thrown away his pick and shovel in favour of learning to fly. A remarkable characteristic about 'Shorty' was his hands, or to be more precise, his little fingers. He didn't have any. Rumour had it that his mining industry Union paid out handsomely for any loss of limb or digit, and 'Shorty' had sacrificed his fingers for the cash. Whether that's true or not, I cannot say, but it was certainly the story he told at the time.

'Shorty' had taken to flying like the proverbial duck to water and was a simply superb pilot who seemed at one with the aircraft he flew. He'd been screened after his first tour, and along with his observer, Flight Sergeant Hicks, had been retained for instructor duties.

The second in this triumvirate was Pilot Officer Gordon Graham, with the inevitable nickname of 'Bluey'. He too was a British subject from Queensland, who had worked in a bank before the war and served in the artillery during compulsory training as a teenager. He was married and much the same age as 'Shorty', and the two came as a pair. He'd flown ops as an NCO and was also a skilled pilot who had a particular passion and aptitude for low level flying which was both exciting and terrifying in equal measure[25].

Completing this merry band was a Scotsman, Flight Sergeant William ('Willie') Caldow. Like the other two he was an exceptional pilot, although at 21 a little younger than the Australians. He had also been decorated with the DFM for his part in the 'Channel Dash' incident and his coolness under pressure would later save my life[26].

---

[25] *David Holford, Graham's CO, wrote that 'Bluey' was '...inclined to be a bit hasty'.*
[26] *The citation for Caldow's DFM reads: On February 12th, 1942, Flt. Sgt. Caldow, as captain of an aircraft, was detailed to attack the German battleships in the English Channel. When the ships were sighted, and anti-aircraft fire was encountered, Flight Sergeant Caldow adopted loose formation and using cloud cover he succeeded in delivering his attack before being intercepted by three enemy fighters. By skillful airmanship the attackers were held off until the rear gunner was able to obtain an accurate sight. One enemy aircraft was then shot down towards the sea and the remainder broke off the engagement. Flight Sergeant Caldow returned to base safely, with his crew intact and his aircraft undamaged. He has at all times displayed a quiet determination and devotion to duty which have been an inspiration to others.*

An Avro Manchester, the less than spectacular forerunner of the war-winning Lancaster.

For a brief period in August the Conversion Flight moved from Breighton to Holme-on-Spalding-Moor. The number of Halifax aircraft on our strength increased to eight, and with it the commensurate number of ground personnel to keep us in the air. I was one of two engineer instructors (the other being Sergeant F Potts) working alongside our pilots and other 'trade' instructors, notably Sergeant Alfred Duringer DFM from Snaith in charge of w/ops and Flight Sergeant Thomas Sankey DFM, who like us was part of 4 Group, in charge of gunnery. Duringer was a particularly pleasant chap who was evidently killing time between tours. He was somewhat flak happy, and couldn't wait to get back onto operations[27].

Potts was rather more of a challenge. He was a heavy drinker, probably to the point of being an alcoholic. Whenever I went to rouse him from his room, he was drunk, and I'd be obliged to take his lectures. He was only ever on time for pay parade!

---

[27] *Alfred Duringer was a Liverpudlian w/op AG who was killed as a flight lieutenant in January 1944 in service with 101 (Special Duties) Squadron. By the time of his death he had added a DFC to the DFM he'd been awarded with 150 Squadron, gazetted in August 1942. He was posted out from 1656 CU in April 1943 to crew with Squadron Leader John St John. Thomas Sankey was awarded the DFM while flying with 35 Squadron. He was later killed in action.*

Humphrey's great friend 'Bluey' Graham with his crew, later in the war. Bluey had a penchant for low level flying.

A huge amount of effort went into converting the Australian crews, work that is largely unrecognised and unrecorded today. The ground crews especially worked tirelessly from first thing in the morning until the light faded in the summer's evening to keep the aircraft aloft, and for the unit to meet its quota of trained pilots and crews. Progress was hampered by the loss of two fully-trained crews on operations in the middle of September and the further loss of one of the qualified pilot instructors, Flying Officer John Purcivall DFC, later that same month. Purcivall, a 30-year old New Zealander, was believed to have been demonstrating the art of a rudder stall when the aircraft spun in from considerable height. There were no survivors from the resultant crash.

'Bluey' and 'Shorty' also almost came to grief on a cross-country when their Halifax suddenly fell into a spin. 'Bluey', as captain, gave the order to bail-out and 'Shorty' needed no second bidding. Happily, 'Shorty' landed safely, and 'Bluey' was able to regain control of the aircraft and land without further incident. 'Shorty' apparently had to put up with some good-natured banter in the mess for several weeks after.

Frustratingly, all of this sacrifice was for nought. In another story that has perhaps not yet been properly told, the Australians decided that they did not like the Halifax and were certainly not going to use it on operations. It was quite simply too dangerous. They were, we believed at the time, close to mutiny. The Wellington may have been outdated, but it was friendly and predictable, especially to new crews. The Halifax was distrusted by pilots, especially for its tendency to develop rudder stall, and the Boulton Paul turrets with which it was equipped were also disliked by the gunners as they were incredibly difficult to get out of in an emergency. The voices of the Australians were clearly heard, and at the start of October 1942, we instructors were converted to Lancasters (the pilots were converted by two pilots from 5 Group) to commence training new crews on yet another new 'type'[28].

My own 'conversion' included ten days at Woodford, at the manufacturing facility of A.V.Roe in Greater Manchester, to complete a dedicated Lancaster 'course'. This was not dissimilar to the course I'd completed in Preston on the Halifax, only better organised. I then took my first flight (in Lancaster W4263) on 9 October, with Squadron Leader Campling at the controls and over the next few days took Willie and 'Bluey' solo as well as taking my first flight in a Manchester (L7460).

By then, however, moves were afoot to further develop our training infrastructure, and create one of the first of the new homogenous Conversion Units.

---

[28] *460 Conversion Flight Diary entry for 25 September, 1942: 'During its short existence, the flight has received many shocks. It was getting used to them now and beginning to weed out the 'duff gen' and the 'gen', and sometimes it is amusing to compare the two and the results. As usual, the flight commander was always the last to get the 'pukka gen'. But on 25th September, as if to soften the news of the previous days, he was able to more than startle the flight with the first-hand news that the Flight were to have the Halifax withdrawn and Lancasters and Manchester were to arrive. Most people took it as a joke, others could not believe our good fortune, but nevertheless it was true.'*

Chapter Four – Heavy Duties

Throughout 1942, the various, squadron-specific Conversion Flights were gradually phased out in favour of dedicated Conversion Units to serve the needs of each Bomber Command 'Group'. The first, 1651 and 1652, met the requirements of 3 Group and 4 Group respectively. Our own unit did not come into being until later in the year as part of 1 Group. Thus, I found myself moved once again without any particular say in the matter!

No 1656 Conversion Unit was formally created on 10 October by amalgamating 103 Conversion Flight (Elsham) with 460 Conversion Flight (Breighton), the latter to become 'A' Flight and the former, 'B' Flight. The Officer Commanding was Wing Commander Arthur Hubbard, who until recently had been the founding OC of 460 Squadron. The two flight commanders were

By the age of 21, David Holford was already a legend in Bomber Command. He and Humphrey were reunited at 1656 CU where S/L David Holford DFC was, by then, a flight commander.

two men with whom I was more familiar: Squadron Leader Campling and Squadron Leader Holford. Within a few weeks we had left our respective bases and moved to a much larger station at Lindholme, near Doncaster in South Yorkshire[29].

Hubbard sent for me not long after we had arrived and there was a short interview. He told me that I was to be promoted sergeant (acting) and put in charge of all flight engineers on the unit as well as being responsible for the

---

[29] *Arthur Hubbard (40050) was awarded the DSO in April 1943. He'd been awarded the DFC in October 1940 as an acting flight lieutenant, a contemporary of the legendary 'Tirpitz' Tait and David Holford. His service number shows that he joined the RAF on a short service commission before the war.*

training of all trainee flight engineers who passed through the station from the OTUs.

The task of training at the Conversion Unit in part mirrored what we had been doing within the Conversion Flights but on a grander scale. It was divided into ground instruction and instruction in the air. Ground instruction was primarily lectures for all of the crew, sometimes together, and sometimes split into their individual specialisms, on such things as day and night landings, three-engined flying procedures, and emergency drill. We would also delve into the specifics of engine performance, throttle, boost, fuel consumption etc.

I did many of these lectures myself, until I had built up and trained a larger team to support me, and found that my previous experience at Halton and St Athan was of tremendous help.

As well as the lecture halls, we had rooms that were equipped with different parts of the aircraft so we could better illustrate how systems worked. To this end, the Section Leaders were left to their own devices: we would scrounge parts from crashed aircraft before the official 'salvage' teams moved in. This allowed me, with the help of our exceptional Chief Ground Instructor (CGI – Squadron Leader Colin Barnes), to commission the construction of a working, diagrammatical fuel system and a fully working undercarriage mechanism so that I could demonstrate the functions of the locking mechanism and the micro switches.

To help me in my task, I roped in the services of two exceptional NCOs. (One was a tin miner from Cornwall who had a catch-phrase – "Never let your prick get harder than your head".) They had both volunteered for aircrew, but I somehow managed to persuade them to defer their service and join my staff. They happily agreed and I was delighted to have their expertise. They drew a series of sketches for the designs, and created a list of parts and spares that we'd need. Some came through official channels, via the stores, others – as I have said – had to be scrounged.

The undercarriage system was particularly impressive and quite a feat of engineering. The design required a transformer to convert 400 volts to 230 volts, to operate the leg, and the whole structure had to be housed in a sizeable rig and suspended on the wall. Other Flight Engineer Leaders from neighbouring stations would come to admire, and were really rather envious.

It was in the air, however, that the fun really began. After a familiarisation flight, the pilots were trained in take-offs and landings (referred to as 'Circuits and Bumps') two at a time, until both pilots were safe to perform solo. Their dual training also included learning how to handle the aircraft with three engines. When it came to the solo, the flying instructor retired to the control tower but the staff engineer (which could be me) remained with the aircraft. It was during some of these solos that I had my hairiest moments.

One story illustrates the point: one night I was with two trainee pilots practicing circuits and bumps and after the first circuit we landed and taxied to the end of the runway for a second take-off. The pilot began running up the engines against the brakes whilst I kept an eye on the instrument panel. To my horror, I could see that there was no oil pressure on the starboard inner engine. My brain took a little while to compute this information and I thumped the pilot hard on the shoulder at which point he mercifully throttled back. I then looked at the instrument panel again and was horrified to see that the starboard inner was showing no revs or boost. Neither pilot had noticed that the engine had in fact stalled (the pilot is supposed to check these instruments as he opens the throttles) and they were about to try and take off on three engines. This would have been fatal. Suffice to say we had strong words afterwards.

I had only been at Lindholme a matter of days before I was on the move again. 'Shorty', 'Bluey' and I took the twenty-minute flight from Lindholme to Wickenby with another 1656 flight engineer, on attachment to 12 Squadron to convert them to Lancs.

The attachment had actually been delayed by a day or two because of bad weather, and the conditions during our stay did not much improve; it was both very cold and very wet, and the strong cross-winds tended to make the three-engined landings especially interesting. Wickenby, a satellite to Ludford Magna, was something of a dump and many of the buildings had in fact been condemned and were due for demolition: we had to cope with leaking roofs and windows, coupled with little or no fuel for the stoves, despite the freezing conditions. The heating issue was resolved in part by my Aussie friends who took down a door or two from other condemned huts and chopped them into firewood. The leaking roofs we tolerated by having a permanent ground sheet on our beds to keep them dry.

We flew in on 13 November, lending the squadron two of our dual-equipped aircraft on which to train. 'B' Flight were the first to be converted, while 'A' Flight continued operating with Wellingtons, patiently waiting their turn.

Within a couple of days, the squadron was officially re-designated a 'heavy bomber' squadron, and dozens of air gunners and flight engineers were posted in to make up the Lancaster's full contingent of crew. Two further instructors also arrived on loan from 103 Squadron to commence the conversion of 'A' Flight[30].

In the event, we completed our task in something of a record time – five weeks – a fact that did not go unnoticed by our superior officers. 'Bluey' Graham received the Air Force Cross (AFC); 'Shorty' Fahey, as an NCO, the equivalent Air Force Medal (AFM). For me there was nothing. Such are the fortunes of war.

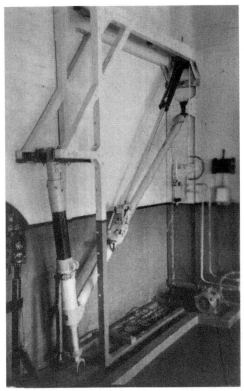

A scratch-built, fully-working undercarriage mechanism enabled Humphrey to demonstrate the functions of the locking system and switches

I quickly built up my hours on the Lancaster to the point that I was able to compare the two aircraft – the Lancaster and the Halifax – based on real experience and with neither fear or favour.

The Halifax was a fairly crude aircraft whereas the Lancaster was more refined in every sense. The Halifax had comparatively poor aerodynamics and certainly didn't fly as well on three engines. The problems with its tail assembly were well documented at the time (and since) and they were constantly modifying the fins to find the answer. She could flip into a rudder stall far too easily and often, catching out all but the most experienced pilots and even some of those lost their lives. There were more technical faults with a Halifax as well as specific 'quirks' like the problems we had with the

---

[30] *The two instructors were listed as Southgate and Crossley*

A diagrammatic fuel system, designed by Humphrey, for classroom instruction

tail wheel; it was even possible for a Halifax to take off and leave its tail wheel on the runway.

When we first started flying the Halifax, engineers were instructed to open the cross-feed cock for the fuel on take-off, and close it immediately afterwards. The idea was that this would ensure that the flow of fuel was constant during one of the most critical phases of flight. Unfortunately, the opposite was actually the case, and leaving the cross-feed cock open actually starved two of the engines of fuel causing the aircraft to crash. I remember clearly the urgent instruction we received to halt this practice with immediate effect[31].

But that was part of the problem with the Halifax: it was too fussy; too unnecessarily complicated. There were too many fuel tanks (the Halifaxes we flew had six fuel tanks in each wing); the hydraulics had too many remedies, and too many things that could go wrong. There were, as I have mentioned earlier, five ways of getting the undercarriage down; the hydraulic power was supplemented by cylinders that stored air under pressure to be used in an

---

[31] *The pilot's notes read: all three cross-feed cocks should be shut off for take-off and also when the aircraft is over the target or over enemy territory where interception is likely. This is necessary in case part of the system should be damaged; if the cocks were open all the engines might cut.*

emergency so in theory we should have been safer, but in practice it just over-complicated matters. Some Halifax flight engineers will no doubt argue that you were fine if you knew your stuff, but it was a great deal to take in, and choosing the right course of action in an emergency, when you are under real pressure, is the difference between life and death.

Everything about the Lancaster was easier: the fuel system was simpler (there were only three self-sealing fuel tanks in each wing); the hydraulic system easier; and the undercarriage less complicated. There was far less to go wrong and therefore it gave you greater confidence when you were in the air. You never heard of a Lancaster falling out of the sky for no known reason, but with the Halifax it seemed to happen with alacrity.

Of course, that's not to say that the Lancaster was perfect. It was not. The flight engineer's position in a Lancaster was as uncomfortable as it was in the Halifax, and ergonomics had not been uppermost in the designer's mind. The flight engineer panel in a Halifax was actually rather well laid out, with the fuel tank gauges, oil temperature gauges, engine temperature gauges etc all logically displayed. The Lancaster flight engineer's position was rather more Heath Robinson, behind and to the starboard of where you stood (or sat if you were lucky) and so less easily accessible.

The Lancaster suffered teething problems with its bomb doors failing to close properly, the front-end jack moving faster than the jack at the rear, as a result of low oil temperature within the pipes that entered at the front and run the length of the bay.

The Merlin XX engines, which powered both aircraft in the early days, also suffered their fair share of problems: water tended to leak through the top cylinder joint which could cause the engine to catch fire. The Merlin XXII had a modified joint and the problem was solved, but the Merlin XXVIII – built in the US – had a different diaphragm-operated carburettor, and the air intake was prone to icing up. This would cause the engines to 'surge' and if not rectified quickly, the engines could be wrecked.

Both aircraft suffered from 'swing' on take-off, and a severe cross wind could aggravate the situation and caused many accidents. It was also very difficult to train new pilots to land the Halifax well. She was a very unforgiving aircraft; if you held off too high you didn't bounce, like you did in a Lancaster. You came down with a crunch, and severely damaged the aircraft. A good pilot if he 'bounced' a Lancaster could actually take-off again, if full power was immediately applied. This was never the case with the Halifax.

Of all the major incidents I experienced, especially when it came to heavy landings, almost every one involved Handley Page's creation. On one particularly foul night, I was with two trainee pilots as they attempted their first solo landings. There was a strong wind on the port beam and the visibility was especially poor. Indeed, the conditions were far from ideal, but these were experienced pilots converting from two engines to four, and so had plenty of hours under their belt.

All was going well on the approach but the pilot slightly misjudged his height as we were hit by a heavy gust of wind which meant that we landed awkwardly. There was a noticeable 'crunch' from the port wheel as all 25 tons hit the runway slightly before the starboard wheel did likewise. As we cleared the runway, I requested that the pilot tell control that we were going to stop immediately, so that I could inspect the port tyre.

Clambering out of the aircraft I looked at the damage with a torch, and found a large gash in the tyre and so reported the aircraft as being u/s. In view of the weather, it was decided we should abandon the exercise rather than transfer to another machine. I wrote up the facts in the Form 700 (the aircraft maintenance record) and we retired to the mess.

The following morning, I received a message that our 'Chiefy' (the flight sergeant fitter in charge of maintenance) wanted to see me out at dispersal. When I got there, he said "I want to show you something," and took me around the side and underneath the aircraft to look at the port wheel. He told me to look specifically at the hub caps. Looking closely, I could see that the caps were badly cracked. Had we attempted to take-off again, the wheel would have broken loose from its mounting and we would have been lucky to have avoided a major crash. Another one of my lives had been used up.

The New Year of 1943 promised to be the final year of the war, or so we hoped. The tide of the war had turned in North Africa, and the Germans were no longer having it quite so easy on the Russian Front. The news was encouraging.

We'd returned to Lindholme on the 15th, during which time the others had been busy. Campling and Caldow had taken two aircraft up to 460 to complete the conversion of remaining squadron crews; and one of our other instructors had been detached to 101 at Holme to complete conversion of four remaining pilots there. Two of our training aircraft, a Lancaster and a Halifax, had been involved in accidents. The former suffered an undercarriage collapse as a result of a heavy landing; the latter an engine failure causing the aircraft to yaw violently, losing height and speed. The instructor assumed control of the aircraft and executed a safe belly landing, and while the crew managed to escape unharmed, the Halifax caught fire and was subsequently written off. There wasn't much of it left for the scroungers to scrounge!

Not all accidents were unavoidable. Some of our instructor pilots liked to indulge in a little low flying when the opportunity allowed, but for one – Flight Sergeant Marks – it proved to be his undoing. His exploits led not only to the serious damage of one of His Majesty's aircraft, but also his Court Martial. He was found guilty of one of two charges and reduced to the ranks.

As aircrew, we were allowed ten days' leave every six weeks, and on Monday 11 January I departed for a well-earned break. With my pass tucked safely in my pocket, I travelled to London by train to stay for five days with my Aunt Ethel (my father's sister) in her flat in Marylebone. Along with my Aunt were her husband Louis, two daughters Joan (25) and Yvonne (21), and Nellie the elderly maid who had been with Ethel's mother as a girl. I took full advantage of being in the capital, taking in four shows and heading out to St Albans for the day to visit Mr Carter, my former boss at the garage.

On the Saturday, I took the train to Leeds to stay with my parents. They had rooms in Mrs Lee's boarding house in Headingly, a prosperous and salubrious part of the city. My sister was also there; she was living in Nottingham at the time and working for Courtaulds. They had been bombed out of their warehouse in Park Royal and moved north. (Within a few months, Eileen was enrolled in the ATS. She subsequently became a radar plotter, posted to the Orkneys.) Once again, I took advantage of the nightlife the city had to offer and ventured into Harrogate to explore. Among the shows I saw was one entitled 'Coastal Command' – something of a busman's holiday.

My leave ended as quickly as it began and I returned to Lindholme suitably rested to find that I'd missed out on two operations to Berlin. Our unit had been asked to provide seven crews on consecutive nights to raid the German capital, the CO and six other pilots taking part including 'Shorty', 'Bluey' and

Willie. Among their number was Flight Lieutenant Hood, and sadly he failed to return from the second trip[32].

I re-commenced flying on 27th, and once again settled back into the routine of air tests and instruction. Campling departed for 460 Squadron, and a new pilot arrived to take his place as Flight Commander, Squadron Leader Johnny Neilson, who I liked instantly[33]. He already had a tour of operations to his name and was now 'resting'. I took my first flight with Johnny on 8 February, one of only a few that month because of a little accident I had on a night out with my two Aussie pals. We'd spent a convivial evening at the local hostelry we frequented and perhaps had one or two more drinks than was thoroughly necessary. We cycled back to camp, arriving shortly before

Humphrey as a pilot officer, prior to his operational tour with his sister, Eileen, who served with the ATS.

the 23.00hr curfew, and as we swung into the main gate I fell off my bike. Brushing myself down I remounted and continued round to the sergeants' mess and made for bed.

As I took my shirt off, in the hut that I shared with 'Shorty', he looked at me quizzically and said: "What's wrong with your shoulder, Phil?" Until then I hadn't noticed much, but on thinking about it agreed that it looked slightly odd

---

[32] *Flight Lieutenant Sefton Hood was a New Zealander, and operationally experienced with 149 Squadron. The navigator that evening was Flying Officer Keith Walter who had taken the place of Flight Lieutenant William Langstaff DFC, the navigation leader. Langstaff, a Canadian, returned to operations with 103 Squadron, being awarded a Bar to his DFC in October 1943. Langstaff survived the war.*

[33] *Campling went on to win the DSO for his part in a daring low-level strike on the Skoda factory at Pilsen on the night of 16 April, a raid in which more than 11 percent of the attacking force was lost. At the end of 1943 he was appointed Chief Flying Instructor at 1 Lancaster Finishing School (1 LFS) at Hemswell as an acting wing commander. He was killed in a flying accident on 8 April 1944, his aircraft crashing at RAF Caistor and bursting into flames. Campling was still only 23 years of age, and had completed around 70 operations.*

and felt rather strange. 'Shorty' agreed: "I think you've dislocated it, mate. We'd better get you over to the Sick Quarters and get them to look at it."

Dutifully I followed, to be met by a somewhat grumpy medical orderly who said he would have to fetch the MO. It was now 23.30hrs and when at last he appeared, and examined me, his manner was brusque and horribly efficient. He proceeded with the 'drill' of putting the joint back where it belonged, and when it came to the final bit, where he swung around with my lower arm firmly fixed in his grasp and the joint clicked back into place, I'm sure I detected a look of unhealthy satisfaction on his face, and not purely for a job well done! Nevertheless, I thanked him profusely and we went our separate ways for hopefully a good night's rest. With my arm in a sling there was plenty of sympathy around, looking as I did like a wounded hero. The sympathy did not last long when I had to admit the true cause of my injury.

We had a change at the top in February. Hubbard's short service commission came to an end and he was transferred to the Royal Australian Air Force Reserve, somewhat unenthusiastically if I recall. He had been a superb commanding officer and we were sorry to see him go, but could not have been happier with his replacement. David Holford was promoted acting wing commander and took over command. Another experienced, decisive and thoroughly likeable officer, Squadron Leader Charles Morton DFC, was posted in to take over 'A' Flight[34].

February saw a steady increase in our strength, including the arrival of nine new flight engineer instructors who themselves had to have some additional training to bring them up to speed. It meant me having to find more space. We were now pretty much in full flow, producing around 40 'new' crews every month, effectively supplying five squadrons within our group: 12 at

---

[34] *Morton won his DFC as a young pilot officer in 1942. Flying with 12 Squadron to Wilhelmshafen on only his fourth operation, his aircraft was attacked by a Junkers 88 and badly shot about. Despite both gun turrets being out of action, his petrol tanks holed, and himself being wounded in the leg, Morton went on to bomb the target and return safely to base. He survived his first tour of operations, winning a second DFC in recognition of his 'exceptional fighting qualities' at a time when just to survive was exceptional. He would later go on to be awarded the Distinguished Service Order, the Station Commander describing him as having 'unflagging enthusiasm, dauntless determination, inspiring leadership and superb skill that few can emulate and none surpass.'*

Wickenby; 100 at Grimsby; 103 at Elsham Wolds; and 460 at Breighton. The elite, the very best of the crews identified, were sent straight to Pathfinder Force which led all of the Main Force raids. Those who failed to pass the conversion course were typically sent to 199 Squadron to stay on two engines for the time being. We also had our fair share of senior officers passing through, often on their way to assume command of a squadron. Among them was Wing Commander Richard Wood, on route to take charge at 12 Squadron, and Wing Commander James Swain, destined to take over 100 Squadron[35].

A well-known danger among trainee pilots and instructors at the Operational Training Units and Conversion Units throughout the war was the quality and reliability of aircraft in which we flew. Seldom did they get their hands on anything 'new'; more usually they were second hand, tired old crates whose airframes and engines had been flogged beyond endurance. Serviceability was an issue, despite the heroic efforts of the ground crews who, it seemed, were fighting a daily battle they could rarely win.

We had many names for such sub-standard and potentially lethal aircraft: some we dubbed 'Friday' machines because they were just built that way; not unusually they were aircraft that had been rebuilt after suffering substantial battle damage. Whatever the reason and whatever the name, they were all 'rogue' kites, pariahs to be avoided at all costs, and you would sympathise with a colleague who was obliged to take one aloft.

'A' Apple was a 'rogue' kite dumped on the unit one morning that had all the hallmarks of being a squadron cast-off. Doubtless they had been delighted to see the back of her. It didn't matter that she couldn't climb above 12,000ft, they probably thought, because we only flew circuits and bumps.

---

[35] *Educated at Dulwich College, Wing Commander Richard Wood DSO DFC won his first award for gallantry in 1940, his award appearing in the same edition of the London Gazette, coincidentally, as a DFC for Wing Commander Hubbard. The DSO followed in late 1943. He retired from the RAF in 1947 and joined the African Affairs Department. He died in Rhodesia in 1969. Wing Commander James Swain arrived at 1656 on 30 December 1942. He was killed in action when his Lancaster was brought down over Denmark on the night of 20/21 April 1943. He was 29. He had been Mentioned in Despatches in September 1941.*

Others completing their training during Humphrey's tenure include Group Captain Reginald Donkin and Wing Commander Donald Craven. Donkin was posted to command RAF Kelstern on completion of his conversion course on 9 September 1943. He had joined the RAF in 1926 and retired in 1952, retaining the rank of Group Captain. He died in 1963. Wing Commander Donald Craven completed his conversion the week earlier, and was posted to 12 Squadron. He was awarded the DFC in June 1944. As Wing Commander D.M.H Craven OBE DFC he retired in 1959.

Willie Caldow and I received instructions to fly the initial air test prior to putting the aircraft into service. We had been told that she had some 'gremlin' in the ailerons and that made us understandably cautious. It was therefore in a thoughtful mood that we made our way out to dispersal via the flight office, where Willie signed the Form 700. We did our external checks – ensuring the pitot head covers had been removed, the cowling and inspection panels were in place, and the leading edge secured – and clambered onboard, wondering what we might find. All seemed to be in order and we commenced our starting, run-up and cockpit drill, blissfully ignorant of the danger at hand.

I checked the temperatures and pressures while the engines warmed up and there was nothing to give cause for alarm. Indeed, everything seemed normal as I checked the magnetos again, each one in turn, and we ran through our take-off drill. Willie opened the throttles to about zero boost against the brakes to ensure the engines were responding properly, and then throttling back he released the brakes and we opened the throttles again gently, advancing the port throttles slightly ahead to counter a tendency to swing to the left.

The Lancaster steadily picked up speed along the runway until we had about 125 mph indicated airspeed and the tail came up. Willie appeared to be lugging on the control column with unusual vigour as he wound back furiously on the elevator trim. He had a strange, somewhat puzzled look on his face as he panted out 'it doesn't want to come unstuck' but spared neither time nor breath for anything more helpful. The runway ahead was fast disappearing beneath us and the hedge marking the airfield perimeter was getting ever closer but there was still no change in note from the rumbling wheels to suggest the aircraft was leaving the ground.

At last, long past the point of no return and with only a few yards to spare, the aircraft reluctantly left the runway and we were finally airborne and in a shallow climb. Quickly this changed to quite a steep climb with Willie now pushing hard on the control column to keep the nose down to build our airspeed and prevent us from stalling[36]. He was furiously winding the trimmer forward again with his right hand to take off all of the trim he had used to get us in the air.

Willie continued to look concerned, though he had now gained sufficient control to produce a normal rate of climb. It was clearly taking it out of him

---

[36] *The recommended speed for a quick climb was 160 mph.*

physically as he instructed me to pull both the wheels and the flaps up to reduce drag and cause a nose-down change of trim. Having complied, he told me that the elevators felt locked and that he had only managed to gain control by an excessive use of the elevator trim control, which I had seen.

It was as we reached 1,000ft that the fun started. Endeavouring to make the first turn to port, onto our left-hand circuit of the station, Willie was again having to use considerable physical force to get the aircraft to do anything. He managed to gasp out a somewhat cryptic message that he felt that the ailerons were now locking, and began frantically winding the aileron trimmer to compensate. It was getting desperate now: 'Think!' he shouted. 'What the hell can it be?'

By now I admit I was scared and finding it difficult to think. I tried to force my mind to work logically and systematically through the possibilities affecting both elevators and ailerons, being overridden by the trim tabs. I could think of nothing, but my thoughts were interrupted Willie's shout that we were not going to make it back to the runway. We needed to find a place to out down, and quickly.

At this point we had achieved a semblance of stable flight. We were able to maintain altitude and speed, and were flying parallel with the runway on the down-wind of the circuit with good visibility. I was therefore able to see the ground ahead and to starboard quite clearly, but alas neither of us could see anything remotely like an adequate piece of flat land on which to make an emergency landing. For as far as the eye could see were the allotments on the outskirts of Doncaster!

A minute or two passed and we were nearing the next turn to port for the cross-wind short leg. Somewhat more composed, Willie quickly briefed me on assisting him on the approach and landing, being unable to release either hand from the control column for fear of falling out of the sky. Rev and throttle levers were mine, as well as all of the other usual duties. Between us we somehow managed to bring the mighty beast back down to earth and even pulled off a creditable landing, all things considered, but as Willie swung us off the runway, he literally collapsed over the control column. Sweat was dripping down his face and he'd turned a shade of grey-green from the exhaustion and shock of the last few minutes. I wondered for a moment whether to call the control tower and request an ambulance but he recovered sufficiently to taxy the Lancaster back to dispersal, raising the flaps and opening the radiator shutters, without uttering a word. There was another long pause at dispersal before switching off all of the booster pumps and finally shutting the engines down.

We spoke briefly about the symptoms and possible causes, and although we still had no real idea as to the root cause, we agreed that the problem was a complete locking of the aileron controls. The other flying controls, and especially the elevators, had also felt odd. Climbing out of the aircraft we jumped into the truck that had been sent by control to collect us and proceeded to the Flight Office for Willie to put the Lancaster u/s (unserviceable) on the Form 700. With that we went our separate ways for a late lunch.

In the sergeants' mess, I joined the only table that was still occupied. A gaggle of my fellow engineers were chatting to a stranger. He was not, as it happens, just 'another engineer', but by some strange quirk was an operational 'type' from a neighbouring squadron. One of my friends commented on my somewhat harassed demeanour, and I was encouraged to give an account of what had happened. Naturally I expected some sympathy, but instead my story was greeted with looks and expressions of disbelief from all except the stranger. With a cynical and rather patronising tone he said: 'It's obvious old chap. You two clots had 'George' in.' His statement was followed by a moment or two of ominous silence, during which time my mind raced over the relevant facts and I had a strange feeling in the pit of my stomach. With something of a cold sweat I spluttered: 'Impossible. Firstly, all of our 'George' controls are wired 'out'; and secondly, it would have been impossible to fly the kite manually with 'George' engaged. We would not be here to tell the tale.'

My statement provoked quite a heated discussion, lasting some minutes. I allowed the others to talk over themselves but made no further contribution to the debate. Instead, I proceeded to bolt my lunch and beat a hasty exit. Grabbing my bike from outside of the mess, I pedalled furiously back to dispersal. Climbing hurriedly into the aircraft and making my way forwards, one glance in the cockpit revealed the awful truth: both of George's clutches were 'in'; the automatic pilot was fully engaged!

Willie and I had just achieved what I had always taught my student engineers was impossible. I recognised immediately I would have to revise my future lectures! Before returning to the mess I spoke to the two riggers who were on trestles, wiggling the ailerons, and suggested that they stopped what they were doing and reported to 'Chiefy'. I got there ahead of them to make my abject confession. When I finally got back to the mess, I quickly phoned Willie and thanked him for saving my life.

The incident was one in which none of us emerged with any credit. We had become so accustomed to our aircraft having 'George' disengaged that we had become careless. The ground crews should have checked before handing us the aircraft; but we should have checked before taking off. All of us had been complacent. We didn't see it because we weren't looking for it. It was a reason for the mistake but not an excuse. We had been lucky, but it didn't do to push our luck too far.

Like all of the Conversion Units and OTUs we suffered our fair share of fatalities in that summer of 1943. Scarcely a week went by without some incident to remind us of the dangers that we faced. Some accidents could be explained; others were more of a mystery. On 23 May, for example, one of our crews disappeared on daylight cross county, never to be seen or heard of again. Somehow they must have become disoriented; had the aircraft come down on land then doubtless it would have been reported. As it was, it must have been lost at sea, most likely the result of poor navigation[37].

A fatal accident the following month was more readily explained. Sergeant Matthew Brown and his crew were on another cross country, this time in the small hours of the morning, when their aircraft collided with a Wellington over Brize Norton and partially broke up in the air. The men in the Lancaster (ED381) were all killed; the crew of the Wellington were more fortunate, all-but the pilot managing to make it out unscathed[38].

This latter incident illustrates another danger we faced. The skies over war-torn Britain were crowded with training and operational aircraft, and our air traffic control infrastructure was still very much in its infancy. The close

---

[37] *The captain of the aircraft was Sergeant Eric Wright, who was reported to have had only four hours flying experience on type. The navigator was Flying Officer Douglas Bishop. The crew is commemorated on the Runnymede Memorial.*

[38] *From 27 OTU. The fact that the crew all made it out in one piece was down to their pilot, Flight Sergeant Mervyn Fettell, an Australian from New South Wales. Fettell stayed at his controls and checked the parachutes of all of his crew before they bailed out. His own parachute pack was missing, and despite frantic searches, they were not able to find it. The navigator believed it had fallen through the front escape hatch. Fettell attempted a landing, despite the starboard engine having completely broken away, but overshot and crashed into trees. The story of Mervyn Fettell's bravery was recounted in an issue of 'Wings', the official publication of the Royal Australian Air Force (RAAF).*

proximity of so many RAF airfields to one another meant we had to keep a constant look-out while in the circuit, not only for our own aircraft, but also aircraft from neighbouring stations.

One afternoon I was out at dispersal, idly watching a Halifax in another circuit a few miles distant. It had caught my eye because it seemed to be behaving oddly. I could tell something wasn't quite right. As I watched, the aircraft appeared to wing over and quite suddenly but dramatically fall out of the cloud. There was a crump and an explosion, followed by a pall of dense black smoke mushrooming in the sky. After every crash, there was a Court of Enquiry to investigate the cause, and on this occasion, it was led by one of our pilots who asked me to assist. We went to the scene of the crash and interviewed an ageing farmer who, in a broad local accent, claimed to have seen the men smoking. Given that he could not possibly have seen whether they were smoking or not at such a distance we dismissed him as an idiot.

There was not much left of the aircraft when we got there, just a large smouldering hole in the ground and a trail of debris. Anything that was still intact had been immediately scrounged by the salvage people or souvenir hunters, and there was certainly nothing to indicate what had caused the aircraft to fall out of the sky in such a fatally dramatic fashion. I was anxious to learn about the conversation between the control tower and the pilot immediately before the crash, but again that revealed little of any value. The whole exercise was incredibly impersonal and I'm not sure we were of any real help. All that we learned was that the pilot was on two engines, that he had stalled and lost control. It was easy enough to avoid as long as you kept sufficient speed and used the rudder to keep you straight. For some reason that we never discovered, this pilot got it wrong.

Tyre bursts, undercarriage collapses, overshoots and undershoots were all par for the course. Most frustrating, however, were taxying accidents as they were usually thoroughly avoidable and unnecessary. Captains could have their log books endorsed for 'carelessness' or in more extreme circumstances, they could even face Court Martial. We had at least three serious taxying accidents during my time at Lindholme including one where the pilot failed to spot a vehicle underneath the wing of his aircraft and his propellers cut into the driver's cab. Happily there was nobody in the front seat at the time or it could have been worse[39].

The second incident had more tragic consequences. It was a night in the late Autumn with two aircraft detailed for night flying. While out on the perimeter track, one of the Lancaster pilots failed to see an aircraft in front and taxied into the rear of another Lancaster, seriously injuring the rear gunner as a result[40].

The third was perhaps the most tragic of all. Another Lancaster was about to take part in a training exercise and was being turned into wind when there was a small bump and a cry from the rear of the aircraft. One of our men, a sergeant by the name of Stiles, had been run over by the tail wheel and killed. It was a terrible and pointless way to die in a terrible and pointless war[41].

For some reason, such tragedies, and the deaths of air or ground crew, did not bother me unduly. Earlier in the war, in 1942, when I was attached to the various Conversion Flights, I distinctly recall returning to 102 Squadron after a few weeks' absence and being notably shocked by the number of missing crews. It was especially noticeable in the mess, and the empty places at the dining tables; cutlery and glasses waiting forlornly for a guest that would never come. Many of the pilots with whom I flew or helped to convert in those early days didn't survive the war; many didn't survive very long at all. Squadron Leader Walkington, Pilot Officer Hunter, Flight Sergeant Harris, Flight Sergeant Peebles, Flight Sergeant Duff, and Flight Sergeant Stone were six 102 Squadron 'types' who failed to return, killed or taken prisoner, some within days of one another. Other pilots in other squadrons shared a similar fate[42].

---

[39] *The pilot in this incident, Flying Officer Jack Murray, had only recently been commissioned and promoted. He was an experienced captain, having won the DFM with 460 Squadron prior to conversion training.*

[40] *The gunner, Sergeant Graham Uttley, died as a result of his injuries.*

[41] *Sergeant Edwin Stiles. He is buried in Streatham Park Cemetery.*

[42] *Flight Sergeant Francis Peebles, a Canadian, was killed in action on 17 June while flying as a second pilot; Fellow Canadian Flight Sergeant Frederick Duff was killed on the night of 25 June on an attack on Bremen; Flight Sergeant Carl Harris crashed into the North Sea in the early hours of the 26 June; Pilot Officer Vic Hunter was shot down on 26 July, hit by flak and obliged to ditch off the German coast. He was taken prisoner; and Flight Sergeant Ronald Stone, a New Zealander, was shot down on 30 July, the victim of a German nightfighter. The last of the group, and the most senior, was also killed in 1942. Squadron Leader John Walkington was killed in action on the night of 3 December.*

Within the training unit, my interest in crashed aircraft tended to be of a strictly professional nature. I wanted to know, if possible, whether the flight engineer had been at fault and could the accident have been avoided. If it had been the result of poor training or instruction, then I would refine my lectures accordingly. We would do everything we could to prevent an accident being repeated.

Not every incident throughout my time as an instructor was tragic, sad or fatal. My efforts in bringing new crews up to scratch may not, until that point, have been recognised with a 'gong', but our CO was appreciative nonetheless and one morning invited me to join him for an early morning run around the perimeter track. It was a particularly cold morning, as I recall, and we had not yet had breakfast. Suitably attired in white vest, blue shorts and gym shoes that had seen better days I did my best to keep up as the wing commander appeared to interrogate me.

What became obvious later was that he was assessing my suitability as an officer and on 11 March I was formally instructed to attend a Commission Board at Holme-on-Spalding Moor. It was the usual affair you would expect: a long table behind which sat four or five senior officers.

I remember little of the actual questions they asked, beyond the obvious around where I'd been to school and what my father did for a living. They were all rather stupid questions and I'm quite sure I gave equally silly answers, but I must have made the right impression for on the 6 May I learned that I had been promoted Pilot Officer (on probation) with effect from 5 April. To celebrate, I had a new Number One uniform made for me by a bespoke tailor in Leeds.

Not long after my commission I walked into the officers' mess one lunchtime and, noticing a stranger at the bar acquiring a drink, I joined him for the same purpose. He was young, his uniform looked new, and he was wearing the badges that suggested he was a doctor so by way of introduction I said: "You must be our new MO?" "Yes," he replied, and introduced himself as we shook hands. We soon got talking and I learned that this was his first appointment. When he told me he came from North London my curiosity got the better of me. When he went on to say that he lived in The Avenue, Willesden, I became very interested indeed.

"Did you happen to know Addie Moses, by any chance?" I asked. To my amazement, he replied: "Yes. We lived opposite Addie and Charlie." This was quite a coincidence; Addie and Charlie were my uncle and aunt. A flash of memory came and I said to him in a dead pan voice: "And you have a sister named Gwen?" "How on earth did you know that?" he retorted. "Because my Aunt told us about her being at the Sea Bathing Hospital…"

As I spoke, I was suddenly struck by a horrifying thought. I could see where the conversation was inevitably heading and could see no possible way of avoiding it. Having started to dig a large hole, I found I couldn't stop! "I was there too, and whenever my Dad came to see me in hospital he always used to pop 'round and say hello…"

I knew at that point that I had 'blown the gaff' as they say, and was probably now in serious trouble. How could I be on active service – and flying – if I had been so ill as to be in a hospital for patients with serious problems with their lungs? There was no retreat and I could only wait for the inevitable denouement. The MO looked at me hard and slightly accusingly. Thoughts were clearly rushing through his head, not least the fact that I had been seriously ill as a child: "What are you doing in uniform and wearing that brevet?" I thought for a moment before replying: "It's a long story," I said, "but I am fit and have passed an aircrew medical." Before he could reply again I added: "It's not likely to prove a problem is it…?"

"No, probably not," he replied, "not if you've got this far without any recurrence. I'm not sure if you could serve overseas, in the Far East for example…" I looked him straight in the eye: "You're not going to tell anyone about this, are you?" I asked. He smiled, and to my immense relief said: "No, I think not." I relaxed and the incident was closed. My secret was safe.

Throughout the spring and summer, we continued to deliver a regular supply of fully trained crews to the front-line squadrons, averaging 40 a month. Bomber Command was going through a difficult patch and new blood was in constant demand. Instructors also came and went: those posted in had typically just been screened, and about to enjoy what was ironically called a six-month 'rest'; the lucky ones posted out were often returning to their squadrons for a second tour, or to a new unit having been promoted to take over a Flight[43].

My logbook for 12 August notes a flight with Captain C P Jones. He was one of three captains and two flight engineers from British Overseas Airways Corporation (BOAC) attached to our unit to learn how to fly the Lancaster. Captain Jones, I later learned, was a highly-experienced pilot who had been the first to fly the North Atlantic Return Ferry Service using modified, unarmed B24 Liberators. I felt there was little that we could actually teach him, and perhaps our time might have been better spent with him lecturing us!

Meanwhile I continued to press our unit commander for an operational posting and he continued to turn a deliberate deaf ear. Although I had flown two operational sorties I did not feel that it gave me sufficient experience to train the men under my command. Some of the flight engineers passing through HCU, especially those with a first tour already under their belts, had considerably more experience than I. Wing Commander Holford, however, seemed keen to convince me that I was too valuable to lose and thus my requests continued to be politely, but firmly, denied.

It was not until the end of October that the CO finally relented. And by then, our Commander-in-Chief had his eye on a new prize. Berlin.

---

[43] *Among those posted in as an instructor in the spring was Flight Sergeant Donald Charlwood – a navigator from 103 Squadron. He was posted almost immediately after to 27 OTU. He later wrote a memorable account of his wartime service - No Moon Tonight - which has since become a classic.*

Chapter Five – Berlin or Bust

626 Squadron pilots including Johnny Neilson (centre in peaked cap).

On reflection, my hankering for a tour of operations could have been better timed. Harris had grown weary of targets in the Ruhr, and switched his attention to Hamburg, a particular favourite of his. The success he enjoyed in the Autumn of 1943, as well as the advent of new technologies and evolution of new tactics and techniques, meant he was now ready for an all-out assault on the German capital. New squadrons were being formed as new aircraft and new crews continued to roll off the literal and metaphorical production lines.

In the last week of October, yet another senior officer arrived at 1656HCU on route to taking command. His name was Philip Haynes, a stocky, broad-shouldered wing commander of considerable experience and expertise. He was a regular Air Force officer who had served on the North West Frontier in the 1930s and was one of the founding fathers of the Indian Air Force (IAF)[44].

Haynes arrived with the rest of the crew from 16 OTU at Upper Heyford in Oxfordshire. Not long after, I was ushered in for another meeting with our

---

[44] *Haynes was one of the early stalwarts of the Indian Air Force with which he flew in the 1930s. He was a flight commander with 1 Squadron IAF, helping to bring newly-arrived pilots up to scratch. After almost four years in India, he returned to the UK with the outbreak of war.*

wingco who had a proposition for me. It transpired that Haynes was going to be the Officer Commanding a new squadron being formed at Wickenby, and was forming a 'crack' crew for the purpose. He had been through the unit's records and specifically requested that I should join his crew as their flight engineer and, if I accepted, then I would also be the new squadron's Flight Engineer Leader.

It was, of course, the usual order of things that crews arrived at Lindholme with most, if not all, of the crew complete, save for the flight engineer and often a second air gunner. In Haynes' case, they were a six who needed to become seven. I was flattered to be asked, and I also learned that Squadron Leader Johnny Neilson, with whom I had accumulated many hours in four-engines, was going to be a Flight Commander and our supplementary captain, when the CO wasn't flying. Haynes would only be allowed to fly so many hours per month, and whenever he was on the ground, Johnny would lead us in the air. Regardless of my feelings towards Wickenby, it was an offer I couldn't refuse and was glad to accept.

Haynes has been described as suave, shrewd and courteous, and I would certainly agree with at least two of those observations. Both Haynes and Johnny Neilson were similar characters: they were quiet, yet confident, and never wasted two words when one would do. In the air, they gave you the utmost confidence that they knew what they were doing, and that was what mattered. Johnny had been a farmer in more peaceful times, and was married. His wife lived in an apartment near Lincoln Cathedral, and as we got to know one another better, we would occasionally be invited out to visit.

In meeting the rest of the crew, I was given that same sense of reassurance that I was in good company. The navigator, arguably the most important member of the crew, was Sergeant Bill Freeman. Bill, a Geordie from Newcastle Upon Tyne and with a broad accent to match, was unflappable, and a first-class navigator who was not afraid to overrule our pilot if he thought he was wrong. A good navigator could save your life; a poor one could equally kill you. Happily, we had the former. Bill worked as a team with the wireless operator, Bob Bond. Bob was also a sergeant and similarly unflappable, but from the other end of the country. He'd been a postman before the war. He was a typical cockney in every sense, and a thoroughly likeable man who had graduated near the top of his course.

The Neilson crew at 626 Sqn. From left: Paddy, Bob, Dick, Johnny, Eric, Bill, and Humphrey in front of Lancaster JB299, Q – Queenie 2.

Completing the trio of men in the front of the aircraft was the air bomber, Eric Simms. Eric was also a Londoner, but from a very different part of town than Bob and with a more privileged upbringing. He was public school educated and thence onward to Oxford, and he had a gift for making friends easily and finding out things about you. A large man, like many in his aircrew category, he had first started out training as a pilot in the US, before being re-mustered and sent to Bombing and Gunnery School in Canada. Perhaps unsurprisingly given his background, Eric had been commissioned by the time he returned to these shores[45].

Of our two air gunners, they were very different characters again. Kevin O'Meara, or 'Paddy' as he was inevitably known, occupied the rear turret and had the frame to suit. Paddy had been in the Jute business before the war, in the small town of Clara in Offaly, southern Ireland. He was very small and equally excitable, and his voice was inclined to rise an octave whenever he became anxious. He also had remarkable eyesight, a rather essential attribute for an air gunner.

---

[45] *Simms won a scholarship to the Latymer School in Hammersmith, where he boxed, played tennis, and rowed in the first eight. He read history at Merton College, Oxford.*

In the mid upper turret was Dick Tredwin, an officer who was not only much older than the rest of us (Dick was in his early thirties) but had also already completed a first tour of operations. A large yet gentle man (he was well over six feet tall), he was pleasant to everyone, a typical characteristic, perhaps, of his west country ancestry. His first 30 ops had been on Stirlings, or as he called them, the 'Queens of the sky'. Most recently he had been a staff instructor at Upper Heyford where the rest of the crew had come together.

In some ways, I was yet again the odd man out; while the others had already formed a bond of trust and friendship, I was the incomer. It was at this time, however, that I acquired my nickname 'Pip', and it stuck, so I was considered an essential part of the crew after all.

With the decision made, we went by road to Wickenby arriving on the 11 November, Armistice Day. The station had changed considerably since my last visit: gone were the dilapidated huts to be replaced by accommodation that was sound in construction and perfectly comfortable. Many of the buildings had only recently been finished by the contractors and there was still a smell of fresh paint in one or two of the rooms.

The station was certainly busy. The incumbent unit, 12 Squadron, had been obliged to surrender one of its existing Flights ('C' Flight) and transfer both its crews and its aircraft to become the nucleus of a new squadron with Wing Commander Haynes at the helm. 'C' Flight 12 Squadron thenceforth became 'A' Flight of 626 Squadron, with Squadron Leader George Roden as its Flight Commander[46].

This was the tried and tested method of forming new heavy bomber squadrons, such that it could be brought to maximum readiness in the shortest possible time. Three-Flight Squadrons were reduced to two, with a complement of 16 rather than 24 aircraft. It was not always easy for the crews who were transferred, since they had already formed their own allegiances and loyalties; conversely it presented an opportunity to create new traditions, and a new esprit de corps[47].

---

[46] *Roden, a New Zealander from Tauranga, was a pre-war officer on the Reserve. His contemporaries in the London Gazette, being promoted from flying officer to flight Lieutenant, include 'Pat' Pattle and Bob Stanford Tuck, two of the war's greatest Allied fighter pilots.*
[47] *According to the 626 Squadron ORB, crews arrived from 1656, 1662, and 1667 HCUs. At least two crews were also posted in from 103 Squadron.*

While Roden had command of 'A' Flight, Johnny Neilson took charge of 'B' Flight, whose ranks were principally filled by ex-conversion unit crews. It was with Johnny that I took my first flight from Wickenby, on 15 November, a short cross-country that allowed us to function as a crew and get to know each other in the air as well as on the ground. It wasn't the best day to go flying: there was quite a bit of cloud about and the rain had a wintry iciness to it. A cross country planned for later that evening was subsequently cancelled, to no great surprise.

I was one of five senior leaders on the squadron in charge of a specialist 'section'. As well as the Flight Engineer Leader, there was also a Signals Leader in charge of all wireless operators, a Bombing Leader responsible for all air bombers, a Navigation Leader in charge of all navigators, and a Gunnery Leader responsible for the air gunners[48]. There was much for us to do in those first few weeks, getting to know the men under our command and being nominally responsible for their good behaviour and discipline. I was keen to monitor the performance of each and every flight engineer on the squadron, taking both a personal and professional interest in their development.

At a practical level, the most time-consuming element of my work came in having to review the flight engineers' logs. Whenever they flew, the flight engineer generated a log of key events. This included a check-list of activities before and after the flight, but more importantly, a record of the amount of fuel used, fuel remaining, air miles, track miles, and the rate of fuel consumption by miles per gallon and gallons consumed by hour. After every operation, these logs had to be on my desk by the following morning (I had a small office to myself) and I had to check and counter-sign each and every one. After a full squadron show, that could mean reviewing sixteen or more such logs, and despatching my findings to Group HQ on a weekly basis. I was not only interested in the fuel efficiency of our aircraft, but also to identify any issues with the flight or the performance of the individual that might need my attention.

Most of my flight engineers, I am happy to say, were willing to comply, and many even took a pride in their work. Only one was particularly troublesome, and that was Sergeant George Walker, the flight engineer in the crew of Jack Currie. Currie was something of a maverick, and for all of his post-war fame, was not especially popular, at least not with me! He was inclined towards

---

[48] *The specialist leaders were: Flying Officer Wood (Signals); Flight Lieutenant Hay (Bombing); Flying Officer William Whitehouse (Gunnery); and Flying Officer Ernest Cappi DFC (Navigation). The latter, an Australian, had won his DFC with 460 Squadron.*

laziness and his discipline was lax, to the point of being foolhardy. A fault with his airspeed indicator, for example, was not reported, and it continued to freeze-up and go u/s. In any crew I had been part of, this would never have been allowed. Unfortunately, the rest of the crew took the lead from their skipper. I recall one occasion his flight engineer appeared in my office at my behest, since he was late in handing in his log sheet. He stood indolently in front of me, without a tie, in what I took to be a deliberate move to provoke me. He should have been immediately up on a charge, but in the event, I let it go; it just wasn't worth the bother. He was caught up in the mirage that Currie was the most important man on the station, even more so than the CO. In punishing the flight engineer I would in fact be penalising the wrong man[49].

The morning of 22 November dawned with a light drizzle, a considerable improvement in conditions over the last 48 hours that had seen a thick fog as our constant companion. We had been stood down for two days and some of the men were getting twitchy. On the one hand, you craved for a rest from the stresses and strains of bomber operations; on the other, and especially for those who were already well into their tours, you wanted to push on to the finish while your luck held. Operations were 'on', and Johnny Neilson was detailed as one of 11 skippers on the Battle Order, the runners and riders for that night's attack.

We were briefed to attack Berlin, tiny pawns in a much bigger game and a promise from our C-in-C to the Prime Minister a fortnight earlier that he could smash the German capital from end to end and bring about the German collapse. He needed the Americans to help him, he said, but in the meantime, we would make a start.

The Squadron Commander, Intelligence Officer, and various specialists ran through the purpose of the raid, our specific aiming points, and other items of interest and detail about flak defences and searchlight belts that might save our lives[50]. It was a major effort comprising well over 700 aircraft, the majority of which would be Lancasters. While the weather over the UK was comparatively

---

[49] *Walker went on to fly a further tour with 582 Squadron, Pathfinder Force, being awarded the DFM in April 1945.*

[50] *Among the Intelligence staff was Michael Bentine, a well-known writer and actor post-war and founding member of The Goons. He had originally volunteered for aircrew but a botched typhoid vaccination almost killed him and ruined his eyes.*

benign, conditions over Germany would ensure their fighters would remain on the ground, and so we were promised an easy trip!

Having donned flying gear over my battle dress in the locker room, the standard Irvin Jacket, fur boots and Mae West in case we came down over the sea and had to swim for it, we left for the parachute section to draw our 'chutes. (The pilot effectively sat on his parachute, which was already attached. This was so that he could remain at the controls and still have a chance of making it out in one piece once the rest of the crew had baled out. The parachutes for the remaining crew were in two parts: the first part was a rather elaborate harness with buckles and two distinct 'clips'. To these clips you would attach the second part of the parachute, which was the parachute pack itself. For those who have never seen or lifted one of these packs, they are deceptively heavy, and you had to be both strong and co-ordinated to attach your 'chute' without assistance. This was all very well on the ground, but in the air it proved to be a challenge to many for some.)

We were also wearing an assortment of undergarments to create 'layers' of warmth. Men began chattering nervously to one another; jokes were swapped with the WAAFs in the stores as the tension began to build. It was palpable then, and for every other operation in which I took part.

We were driven out to dispersal in a series of trucks, buses, and other four-wheeled vehicles that were to hand, men jumping out as they came to their 'stop'. Johnny had his own vehicle, a Standard truck. On our 'pan' was Lancaster JB599 UM - Q2 – known affectionately as 'Queenie two'. She had been fresh from the factory only days before, and we were pleased to have her. Given that we were the senior crew, 'Queenie two' would become our regular 'mount'.

Before climbing in, we ran through the usual visual checks, checking for visible signs of fluid (i.e. hydraulic, oil, fuel etc.) leaks, that the cowlings were secure and the pitot head cover was removed. The latter was especially important; it was an open-end tube that supplied the air pressure for the air speed indicator to work. (Put another way, if you left it on, you would have no idea how fast you were flying, and that made things like landing rather dicey!) Once satisfied, we waited until it was our time to move. Getting a large number of aircraft into the air in the shortest time possible required considerable organisation, and the take-off procedure was carefully timed so that we would be ready to move off as soon as we received the green Aldis signal from control.

79

One last ritual was the traditional urinating on the tail wheel, a practice that most crews executed at the time. It was part superstition, part tension, and part a practical need for it would be a long flight to Berlin of seven hours or more. Although we had an Elsan chemical toilet on board, it was rarely used. It meant disrobing several layers of clothing for one, and for another, it meant abandoning your position which we were not wont to do except in an emergency. (The practice continued until the Air Ministry issued one of its orders that stated that the result of our 'promiscuous urination' was '…damaging corrosion which is quite unacceptable!')

At last our skipper would break the spell and give the nod to board the machine which we did from the rear of the aircraft. For the rear and mid upper gunners, this meant only a short trip to their positions; for the rest of us, it meant clambering along the length of the Lancaster, and over the main spar. Each of us was alone with our thoughts, niggles and worries. I was always worried, for example, that the four Merlins would start without difficulty and that they would perform well on the 'run up' test. A failed engine now would mean an immediate transfer to another machine, if it were available, or for our operation to be scrubbed altogether which none of us wanted.

While I busied myself with my duties, and checked that my lucky pencil was safely onboard, the rest of the crew dealt with their own concerns, the navigator and wireless operator setting out their charts and flimsies and the air bomber looking over his sight and computer. In our case, the skipper was always the last to take his seat at which point the ground staff took up their positions. Johnny and I went through the lengthy cockpit drill as we had done dozens of times before, ensuring the engine controls were set in their pre take-off positions. Then we were ready for start-up, and the skipper signalled that he was ready to get underway. The starter buttons were pressed as the ground crews worked the priming pump as the first engine caught and then burst into life. Within a few moments, all four engines were alive and the ground crews withdrew, their task complete.

For me at this point, there was a sense of relief. I switched off the booster-coil switch and, between the skipper and I, we opened each engine up slowly to 1,200rpm to warm up. It took several minutes for the temperatures and pressures to reach the desired levels and we completed further tests such as raising and lowering the flaps to ensure the hydraulics were in order. Another check list was completed before we were at last cleared for taxying, and we began to make our winding way from our dispersal to the end of the runway, keeping a safe distance from the aircraft in front in the mounting gloom. It was the late afternoon, and already pitch black.

The cockpit was cramped, noisy, and uncomfortable. There was no soundproofing or wall covering; there was bare metal everywhere, freezing to the touch, and the upholstery, such as it is, can best be described as utilitarian. With the four Merlins now belting out power at 1,600 rpm, speech was impossible, other than via the intercom. There was limited space in which to move, and the length of our intercom lead and oxygen tube also restricted our sphere of operation. Both had to be disconnected to move aft, and that could be troublesome. Above 10,000ft, and it meant using one of the portable oxygen bottles with a 10-minute supply.

The only time I sat (using the second pilot's seat) was during take-off and landing, which meant for the rest of the flight I would be standing. So, although we were issued with a flask of coffee, a bar of chocolate, and even – occasionally – some tinned orange juice, this was no pleasure cruise.

I logged our take-off time at 16.55. The Lancaster was bloated with fuel and bombs and there was always a balance to be struck. We needed fuel to reach the targets furthest away, but that meant sacrificing bombs, because we could not exceed an all-up weight. I noted in my logbook the weight in lbs: 64,000. We were carrying a 4,000lb High Capacity bomb and a huge number of 30lbs and 4lbs incendiaries. The big bomb was designed to blow the roofs off, and the incendiaries would then create a fire and burn what was left. The Lancaster needed all of the runway to come unstuck, and once again there was a sense of relief as the undercarriage came up and the lights winked to show me it was locked.

The journey out was uneventful on a track over the North Sea and crossing the Dutch coast for a direct route to the north of Hannover and straight to Berlin. Although it was tremendously cold outside, I was comparatively warm at my post. We were in heavy cloud virtually all of the way which was both a comfort, because it meant we were hidden from the German defences, but also a potential danger, because of icing. A build-up of ice on the leading edge of your aircraft altered its flying characteristics so dramatically that you could easily stall and crash. Pitot tubes could also become blocked, rendering the ASI useless.

As we passed Hannover, the first of the flak appeared, but a little way off. The 'nastiness', as we called it, could start at any time, often just as we crossed the enemy coast. The Germans had strength in depth to their defences, and seemed to increase in ferocity as our tour progressed. We had measures to counter German nightfighters, such as 'Window' which disrupted their radar control, and devices like 'Monica' and 'Fishpond' to detect when a fighter was nearby, but little or nothing to counter the flak other than our wits, good flying, and luck[51].

Flak was always something to be feared and respected. Sometimes it was 'predicted' flak. Whereas light flak exploded in impact, heavy flak had a fuse to enable the moment of explosion to be predicted. If the gunner could estimate the height and position of your aircraft, he could adjust the fuse in such a way as to register a hit. Even a near miss could bring you down, such was the force of the explosion.

We could be flying along in clear sunshine or dark cloud, and all would seem peaceful. Then, quite suddenly and without warning, we'd see an explosion, perhaps 500 or so yards to starboard. Perhaps it had not found its target, but occasionally there would be a bright flash followed by one or two smaller flashes, and then flames as an aircraft was hit and began falling out of the sky. We would then see a trail of fire and watch it, almost transfixed, for maybe upwards of 20 or 30 seconds before at last there was another explosion and another burst of light as the aircraft hit the ground. We assumed always that it was one of our aircraft that had been hit, but in the cloud, it was difficult to tell. Indeed, when shrouded in a blanket of 10/10th cloud, it was almost impossible to know with any certainty what we had just seen. There was rarely any comment from the crew and the flight would continue, moving deeper and deeper into the hostile sky and the possibility of an enemy fighter.

We reached the outskirts of Berlin unscathed and prepared for the bombing run. Another note was entered into my log, and I continued to keep a keen eye on the engine dials.

Johnny spoke to the gunners again and told them to keep their eyes peeled.

---

[51] *The Germans re-organised their flak defences throughout 1943 to create concentrated 'Grossbatterien' or 'large batteries' to protect all large and important targets. They also increased the size and calibre of weapons available, beyond the famous 8.8cm guns to include 10.5cm guns and even the first 12.8cm artillery pieces. The 8.8cm could fire a shell of approximately 20lbs at a rate of 12 rounds per minute up to 25,000ft; the larger calibre 10.5cm could fire an even heavier shell (c32lbs) at a rate of 10 per minute up to 30,000ft. While Window had seriously disrupted their nightfighter capabilities, the Germans continued to increase the weight of flak opposition through to the summer of 1944.*

They continued to scan the night sky for any hint of danger. A shadow. We were in a stream, and a stream offered protection, but there were often stories in the mess of our aircraft being attacked on their bombing run, when the aircraft was obliged to fly straight and level for several minutes to ensure the bombs could be dropped as accurately as possible. On the approach, the nastiness increased dramatically. There were bright flashes everywhere, alongside brilliant white parachute flares that illuminated the night sky. It was not clear whether they were our own flares, dropped by the Pathfinder crews responsible for marking the target, or those of the enemy, to silhouette our aircraft against the cloud.

An aircraft received a direct hit from a flak shell and exploded spectacularly in mid-air. Johnny began a series of long turns and climbs, a weave to throw off the predicted flak and the fighters, and to give our gunners a greater chance of spotting the enemy before he had us in his sights. He could not do this for long, however, because we must make our attack. Eric made his way into the bomb aimer's compartment in the nose, as Zero Hour approached. He switched on the computer and the gyro on the Mk XIV bombsight, and effectively took command of the aircraft.

There was the occasional buffeting of the aircraft as we found ourselves in the slipstream of an aircraft ahead, although we could not see it. A shell exploded close by, but happily not close enough and we continued our relentless journey to the target. The Pathfinders were late, but at last Eric was satisfied and after a series of instructions to the pilot he called 'bombs gone' and the aircraft lifted as the weight from her belly was released. Eric confirmed that all of the bombs had indeed fallen, and that we had no 'hang ups', before the bomb doors were closed and Bill called out a course to steer for home[52].

First, we had to clear the target area and Johnny almost immediately started to weave again, and called for more power. There was an abundance of colour both in the air and on the ground: bright flashes of white and yellow and dripping markers of red and green, adding to a scene of pyrotechnic chaos. It seemed impossible that any of us could survive and Bill emerged from behind his curtain to see what the fuss was about. It was the one and only time he ever came to look.

---

[52] Cookies' – the 4,000lb cylindrical bombs – were especially prone to 'hang-ups' and failing to release. Among the various controls at the air bomber's disposal was a switch for a heater to prevent the bomb from icing up.

We were now through the target and on the return leg. This was still a dangerous period and there was no time to relax. The cloud had rendered the searchlights virtually useless but they still tried to find us in the dark. It was as though we were being chased away, and I afforded myself a look down to see a number of huge explosions on the ground. Later, Johnny would report that aircraft were attacking from all manner of headings and as such the bombing appeared scattered but at the time I simply marvelled at the destructive power we had wreaked. We expected to see route markers on our return (there had been a number on our route in) but none were seen, and we were left to the skills of our navigator to bring us home unaided.

More than seven hours after leaving Wickenby and being waved off by the faithful ground crews we were now in the circuit and waiting our turn to land. We were still alert. Intruders had been known to lie in wait of returning aircraft and shoot them down in sight of home. Johnny had called up flying control and given our runway on which to land. It was ten past midnight as our wheels touched the earth in a copybook landing and we taxied back to dispersal to shut down. There was the usual resentful crackle and pop from the engines as we switched off, and at last scrambled out with a promise of a debrief and our post-op eggs and bacon.

We went to Berlin twice more that month. On our third trip, we had Wing Commander Haynes in the pilot's seat and we were obliged to divert to Dalton on our return because of foul weather. There was little to report other than being coned by searchlights over the target, which gave us all a scare. Berlin was not covered by cloud, as we had been promised, and that allowed the searchlights to play. One of our crews was missing, and two more crashed on landing[53]. Neilson was back in command for our final two raids of 1943, a further attack on Berlin on 16 December and a new target, Mannheim, on the night of 20th. The latter was only significant as it was not a 'Main Force' effort but rather a diversionary raid to steer the nightfighters away from the 'real' target, Frankfurt. We flew in and out with nothing to trouble us.

Trouble, however, was never far away.

---

[53] *This was a bad night for 626 Squadron. Flight Sergeant Cecil Kindt, a 21-year old Canadian, and his crew failed to return, nothing being heard after take-off. Flight Sergeant Keith Windus RAAF overshot and crashed while trying to land at Marham in Norfolk. All of his crew were killed. A third aircraft, flown by Flight Lieutenant V Wood, crashed at Lissington. The aircraft was destroyed, although the crew emerged unscathed.*

Chapter Six – A Long Hard Slog

Christmas came and went with the threat of an operation that was subsequently cancelled allowing us to celebrate in peace with a football match against 12 Squadron. Squadron Leader Roden went missing on a trip to Berlin earlier in the month, and his place as Flight Commander was taken by 'Bill' Spiller[54].

One of my more unusual duties as Flight Engineer Leader was to be the Squadron's Air Sea Rescue expert, for which additional training would be supplied. In addition to devising and delivering specific lectures on the subject (for example around search procedures, lifeboat coverage etc), I was also required to actively encourage crews to practise their ditching drills and time them doing it. Some of the training was done on their usual aircraft, and other parts in a water tank built for the purpose.

I thus spent the first week of the New Year in Blackpool, but rather than enjoying the sea and the sand, I spent my sojourn on an Air Sea Rescue course, trying to consolidate and bring to life my existing knowledge of the subject. Alas, I was billeted with a chap who was more interested in beer and girls than the content of the course, and was rather led astray, to the point that the session in a dinghy in the Irish Sea was beyond me owing to a riotous time the night before.

I did, however, have rather more success with the simulated parachute jump into the international standard swimming pool. This required me to jump feet first from the top diving board in full flying kit including boots, Mae West, and parachute harness. I made my way somewhat uncertainly to the top of the board and peered over at the drop for what seemed an eternity before finally taking the plunge. I had never jumped more than a few feet previously and it looked an awful long way. As it happens, it was much easier than it looked and I actually enjoyed it. I learned quite a bit from the course, and returned to Wickenby confident of being able to teach our crews a thing or two about survival.

We flew five operations in January, four of them to Berlin and the fifth to Brunswick for a change of scene and less success. Eric had the unusual

---

[54] *Squadron Leader Josiah 'Bill' Spiller was a remarkable character who completed his first tour of 28 operations as an air gunner in 1940/1941. He subsequently trained as a pilot in Canada, returning for a second tour, first with 7, then 625 and finally 626 Squadrons. He survived the war and returned to civilian life as a solicitor. He died in 1980.*

distinction on 20th of firing-off a few rounds from the front turret at a passing Dornier 217, but didn't claim to have hit it. We also took some flak on the raid on 27th, and our instruments rendered u/s.

Flight Sergeant Keith Margetts.

We lost four crews, though compared to some squadrons in this period our losses were slight[55].

The weather in the first two weeks of February was poor, and we were stood down for several days. During daylight hours, we were kept busy with films and lectures, and chance to catch up with any outstanding paperwork. A number of new crews were posted in to replace those we had lost or who had completed their tours, and each were lectured on the Lancaster fuel system and engine handling before taking part in a Command 'Bullseye'.

We flew just the two operations, another trip to Berlin and one to a different target, Augsburg, to attack the famous Diesel-engine works. On the first, we took a second pilot, Flight Sergeant Keith Margetts, along with

---

[55] *Flight Sergeant Kenneth Elkington and Pilot Officer Norman West were lost on the attack on Brunswick (Braunschweig); Flight Lieutenant Noel Belford RAAF and his crew were killed in action on the night of 27th, shot down by a night fighter on their homeward leg. Only one of the crew, Flight Sergeant Arthur Lee, survived to become a PoW. They had survived a ditching only a few weeks before on their return from Stettin, ironically while Humphrey was away on an Air Sea Rescue course. They had been rescued by HMS Midge; Flying Officer John Wilkinson and his crew failed to return from operations on the night of the 30th. These losses do not tell the whole story, however. The crew of Yorker Two, captained by Flying Officer Bill Breckenridge, also had a dramatic night on 30th. They were attacked by a nightfighter and the wireless operator killed on the first pass. Both gunners were also hit and the navigator severely wounded. (Page 21 of Appendices). Breckenridge was wounded in the legs but recovered quickly and features in Humphrey's log book for a flight in April, a turret test. He went on to complete his tour and serve as an Air Traffic Controller at Glasgow Airport until his death in 1971.*

A publicity photo with Humphrey (far left) and crew. Spiller and Neilson are standing centre.

us on what was called a 'Second Dickey' trip to give him first-hand experience of a bomber operation prior to leading his own crew. As he had never been on an operational sortie before, through no fault of his own he served little purpose other to get in the way and make an already cramped cockpit even less comfortable[56].

On the second, we had the Squadron Gunnery Leader, Flight Lieutenant William Whitehouse, join us in the rear turret. It was a bitterly cold flight, with a route that skirted neutral Switzerland. We saw a good explosion or two below us, but the markers had difficulty because their target indicators were quickly extinguished by the snow! This was not in fact the only time that Whitehouse came along for the ride. I remember him for an incident in which I displeased him and he had every cause to be angry with me. I'd flown a gunnery exercise in the rear turret and not long after we landed he asked to see me. He told me in no uncertain terms that I had committed a terrible offence. I had left a bullet up the spout! In all fairness to the man he was right to admonish me, for it was equally stupid and dangerous, and could have caused serious harm. Needless to say, I never did it again!

---

[56] *The 'guest' was 21-year old Sergeant Keith Margetts. Margetts later went on to captain his own aircraft, and was shot down and killed on the night of 24/25 March on a trip to Berlin. Group Captain Haynes described Margetts as being courageous and capable.*

A happier event also occurred in February, when the whole squadron, including ground crews, and its aircraft were lined up for a publicity shot. In a now-famous photograph, I can be seen standing in a small group towards the back, with Johnny Neilson on my right. Eric is stood at the very back on his own, with only the Wing Commander for company!

I had a break from operations in March on account of being sent away on a Flight Engineer Leader's course. It meant a return to St Athan, and it proved to be a colossal waste of time. The Chief Instructor, a Flight Engineer though with the rank of Squadron Leader, wanted to know why I was so disengaged and failing to mix with my fellow students. For one thing, I didn't welcome the interruption to my tour, and for another, I found him as unacceptable as the so-called training he delivered. The course was designed for flight engineers who had not yet been section leaders, whereas I had been doing the role for two years. I resented someone teaching me who knew less than I did![57]

Nonetheless, I did not excel, and was given a 'B' pass which, in the circumstances, was probably fair. My behaviour, on reflection, was stupid and childish, but if I had held more respect for this man's abilities and suitability for the role, jointly we might have had a more profitable experience. It was a blessed relief when it was all over and I could return to operational duties.

I flew to Berlin on no fewer than nine occasions during our tour and came through unscathed when many didn't. By the start of April, I was already half way through my allotted 30, notching up my 15th operation with a different pilot, Bill Spiller. As the Flight Engineer Leader, one of my roles was filling seats with 'spare bods', when a member of a particular crew was sick, on compassionate leave, or otherwise unavailable. Some Leaders chose to fill those seats themselves, though I was always a little more circumspect and would only ever fly with pilots that I trusted. Bill Spiller certainly fitted into this category, a fine airman who never once gave cause for alarm. He was in

---

[57] *Humphrey's log book suggests his Nemesis was Squadron Leader Rennie. This is possibly Claude Andrew Rennie DFM ex-214 Squadron. The crew flew two operations while Humphrey was away, his place being taken by Pilot Officer Henderson. Both operations were to Frankfurt.*

the same mould as Johnny, the wing commander, et al, and those I had been lucky enough to fly with in my early career.

These men all seemed to have strong reserves of courage to match their skills at the controls. To use the parlance of the day, they were 'press-on' types. Courage is that quality that enables people to meet danger without giving way to fear; fear, conversely, is defined as a normal human reaction when faced with a situation perceived as threatening one's life. The RAF in the second world war had an irregular way of dealing with men who lacked the courage or allowed fear to get the better of them. They called it 'Lack of Moral Fibre' (LMF) when one had sacrificed the confidence of one's commanding officer. I have little knowledge of how the victims of LMF were treated, beyond the point of disclosure. Some COs, I understand, were sympathetic and would arrange a discreet transfer with the minimum of fuss; others liked to make an example of LMF cases, to prevent it from spreading to others in the squadron.

Certainly, those raids on Berlin on the winter of 1943/44 pushed men to the very limit of their endurance. The loss rates on some of the raid were appalling, and very quickly men worked out that if those rates continued, they stood no chance of completing their tours. They would be dead, or at best a prisoner of war, well before their '30' was up. I did not take part in the raid on Leipzig in February when we lost 78 of our bombers, and was at St Athan during the attack on Nuremberg, in which we lost close to 100[58].

For my part, I was scared every time I took to the sky, and was never more comfortable than when all three wheels were back on the runway. It was especially scary when 'Bluey' Graham insisted on beating up the 'drome, which he was wont to do on occasion, after we had completed most of our air tests, though the fear of getting reported was probably greater than the fear of coming to grief. Operations were frightening in their own way, for obvious reasons, and curiously, experience did not consciously lessen the degree of fear I actually felt. It is clear that those who showed no fear engendered confidence in the rest of us; imagine the opposite, and you have the likely explanation for the number of early returns, or crews jettisoning their bomb loads short of the target.

Chance, of course, also played a key part in our survival. At the time, many of us were inclined to the view that it was all a matter of luck, but we did not then have the relevant statistics (later available) to provide a clue to our chances. I did not know, for example, that when the conversion unit changed from flying

---

[58] *On one occasion, 12 Squadron lost four crews in a single night.*

The remarkable sight of a Cookie falling from a Lancaster's bomb bay.

the Halifax to the Lancaster, that my chances of surviving had improved by a significant amount. In a similar vein, I was unaware at the time that by being crewed with Philip Haynes' 'hand-picked' team, I was similarly improving my chances by a worthwhile percentage.

I am not aware that anyone with any degree of authority has made an academic study of chance within the context of Bomber Command operations over enemy territory during the war. There are, however, statistics that forecast your chances of survival, commensurate to the number of operations flown, and it is interesting to see how these ratios changed as the war progressed. A friend of mine who was also a flight engineer was returning to base, having successfully concluded a trip, but with his aircraft somewhat damaged in the process. They crashed during landing and the aircraft split into two: the rear and mid upper gunners and the wireless operator all to the aft of the split were killed; my friend, the navigator, the air bomber and the pilot, all survived, although some badly injured. That is chance.

So too is an incident of our own while returning from the raid to Berlin on 15 February in which we had been hit by flak. We were on our way in to the target when Bill, our navigator, announced on the intercom calmly that we were just about to enter into an area that was marked on his charts as having a known flak concentration. Just as the words came out of his mouth, there was a terrific bang close to our starboard port quarter, immediately followed by a rattle right next to me, behind my instrument panel. Instinctively I looked at the gauges and was shocked to see that every one of them was showing a maximum reading.

In theory, I should have feathered all four engines, but my experience told me that the fault lay elsewhere, and that it was probably electrical. Recognising that gauges go 'up' and not 'down' when the current is cut, I conjectured that something must have severed the wiring behind the panel. Seeing something on the floor I flashed my torch under the panel to find the likely culprit – a small lump of metal. Instinctively I reached down to pick it up and promptly dropped it straight down again as it burned a hole in my white silk glove. (We always wore silk gloves in preference to mittens to get a better 'feel' for the controls.) The cause of the damage was a sliver of red-hot shrapnel.

That piece of shrapnel had missed me by less than a foot; another piece missed the bomb aimer, Eric, by a matter of inches. I was of course unable to fix the fault while we were in the air and so had to do some intelligent guesswork. I figured that we might well be losing fuel, and so balanced the tanks on the opposite side to where we were hit, just in case. We flew back on dead reckoning and made it home without further incident. I was given my piece of shrapnel as a souvenir by the ground crew after we landed.

Chance could therefore kill you, or spare you. Skill and experience, on the other hand, as well as the ability to recognise danger could save your life. A good navigator, for example, would get you home; a poor one might have you over the target too early, and needing to dogleg to return to the stream, or find you lost over the sea. And you'd be dead. When I failed, at the Conversion Unit, to check that George was locked out, my pilot saved us both. That's why being part of a crew was so important[59].

Berlin was dangerous. Its defences could be lethal. It was actually on the return from a different target, however, that we came closest to getting the chop.

---

[59] *Experience, of course, was not always enough. On the night of 24/25 February, Flight Lieutenant Jack Hutchinson DFC RAAF and his crew were shot down on the final trip of their first tour. He was also carrying a 'Second Dickey', Sergeant Bryan Bowditch. Hutchinson had already survived an earlier ditching in which two of his crew had been killed.*

Chapter Seven – Friendly Fire

It was late afternoon on 26 April when we wandered into the briefing room to learn that our target for tonight was Essen, in the Ruhr. There were the usual groans from the more experienced crews who recognised the 'Happy Valley' as being the graveyard of many of their contemporaries. But at least it wasn't Berlin. The trip before we'd attacked the marshalling yards at Aachen, and Essen promised to be another, shorter flight, but rather more dangerous.

The Battle of Berlin was over. Now our efforts were being directed against targets that would support the imminent invasion of Europe that was planned for the late Spring. Operations were being dictated by an even higher authority than Sir Arthur Harris and we were obliged to obey, although it was noticeable that in giving his full support to the directions received, he still liked to apportion some of his bombers to more familiar targets whenever he could. This was one of these occasions.

Essen involved an attacking force of nearly 500 aircraft and our take-off was not scheduled until after 22.00hrs so we had quite a time to wait, which only increased the nervous tension. It was a full squadron show for us, with 16 aircraft taking part[60].

We were allocated a different aircraft for the raid, LL798 – Nuts 2, which was again a relatively new Lancaster. We'd loaned our regular kite, 'Queenie Two', to another pilot and his crew and they'd failed to bring it back[61].

We were over the target by 01.31hrs and Johnny Neilson had managed to get 22,000ft out of our new aircraft despite a heavy bomb load that included the obligatory 'Cookie' and over a thousand small incendiaries. In the nose, Eric had a good view of the target and the Pathfinder Target Indicators. Up to that point it had been a textbook raid. Eric called 'Bombs Gone' and then it happened.

---

[60] *The Bomber Command force that night was split between Schweinfurt and Villeneuve St Georges.*

[61] *Lancaster JB599 was lost on operations to Frankfurt on the night of 23/24 March. The captain, Flying Officer George Kewley, and his crew were all killed. They included 18-year old air gunner Sergeant William Dixon, one of the youngest aircrew to be killed on operations in 1944 and indeed for the whole of the war.*

The first I knew that there was trouble was when a tremendous shudder seems to run through the Lancaster. It was clear that we'd been hit but where and how was not immediately apparent. Johnny went through the usual emergency procedure of calling up the crew to check that we were OK. Each replied in turn with a simple acknowledgement, but there was no response from the mid upper gunner, Dick Tredwin. Again, and in accordance to the drill, he asked me to make my way aft to find out what was wrong.

I unplugged my intercom and oxygen mask and grabbed one of the portable oxygen bottles. It was easy enough to fit around your neck with the gauge at the front so you could monitor the supply. Ten minutes could pass very quickly. I squeezed past the navigator at his table, and beyond him under the astrodome and the wireless operator's station to the main spar, the joint at which the fuselage and the wings came together. Clambering over it in full flying gear was no mean feat, but we learned to be agile while moving about in a Lancaster.

I came at last to the mid upper position and could see Dick, in his turret, seemingly unconscious, slumped across the breech of his guns, and with his head shorn of its helmet. More urgently, his face mask had also been ripped away, and he was without oxygen. His turret canopy was badly smashed, and he was largely exposed to the elements. At the same time, I felt, rather than saw, that we had been holed somewhere between the turret and the rear exit door.

My immediate thought was to release Dick from the turret, and I started to unclip his seat (he had a seat much like a children's swing). Dick, however, was a well-built man and a dead weight, and I very quickly realised that with our size difference I had no chance of getting him out alone, not without potentially causing considerable damage to the pair of us. I quickly abandoned that idea, until I could get further aid.

I went a little further aft, and shone my torch to see where the gale was coming from and the extent of the damage. I was somewhat horrified by what I saw: a 200mph wind was blowing through a gash around four feet square on the port side, near the flare chute. It was all I could do to remain standing, such was the power of the slipstream. The control columns for the ailerons and rudder were exposed, and whatever had hit us had missed these vital arteries by a matter of inches. The object (or objects) had carried on through the fuselage, peeling its skin backwards like a giant tin opener, and wrecked the flare chute before exiting the aircraft. Had we been hit a few seconds earlier, before the flares had been dropped, it would doubtless have ignited them and I would not have lived to tell the tale.

By now my oxygen was getting low, and so I plugged into one of the local ports for additional supply. I also plugged into the intercom to make my report. Johnny was never keen on anyone being on the intercom for too long, especially over enemy territory, and so ordered me back to my flight station. It was a very tense atmosphere, and back in the cockpit I assessed whether any other damage may have been caused by debris to the fuel, hydraulic or electrical systems but all appeared to be performing on the top line and Johnny still had good control of the aircraft.

The danger now was hypoxia as Dick was being starved of oxygen. This would cease to be a problem below 10,000 feet and so Johnny lost height as quickly as he could, albeit mindful of the damage to his aircraft. As the altimeter reached 10,000ft, Johnny instructed me to go aft again, and to take Eric with me in case I needed help. (Having already dropped his bombs, Eric was really the only man who could be spared.) We again made our way to the rear of the aircraft, sweating as we did so despite the cold, but this time there was a further surprise. As we reached the mid upper turret, Dick wasn't there! It is difficult to convey just how disconcerting that was, to be fumbling around in the dark confines of a Lancaster, with nothing but the pathetic beam of a pocket torch to light the way, and to find one of our crewmen had seemingly disappeared!

All manner of thoughts raced through my mind, not least that he had somehow been sucked out of the aircraft by the slipstream. Given the size of the hole, I figured it was not unfeasible. The intensity of the situation, the physical effort, and the lack of oxygen dumbed my sense a little, but common-sense ultimately prevailed and I realised he couldn't have gone far. I thought he must have regained consciousness and made his own way out, and was probably further back in the aircraft. And so it proved.

We found Dick, who had lost consciousness again, slumped against the fuselage side, forward of the exit door. In his physical and mental state, he may have reasoned that we had been fatally hit, and that the skipper was about to order us out. On close inspection, we could see that he'd received a nasty blow to the back of his head, around the ear, and that it was bleeding. It was agreed that it was better to leave Dick where he was, rather than attempt a hazardous move to the sick bed, and I left Eric in charge of dressing his wound with the first aid kit. I was needed back at my station.

It was a long and somewhat fraught flight back to Wickenby, as there was always the thought that there might be other structural damage that we couldn't see in the dark. We called ahead for a priority landing, and were told that the ambulances and fire tenders were standing by. As it was, Johnny pulled off an excellent landing, and we were quickly surrounded by the emergency services who helped carry Dick from the aircraft and into a waiting blood wagon. We did not have the facilities to look after him at Wickenby, his wound was too serious, and so he was obliged to take a doubtless uncomfortable journey by road to the RAF hospital at Raunceby where he could get the proper medical attention he required.

Fate had spared Dick Tredwin that day but it had not always been so kind. Only a few months earlier, in December, his wife Beryl had died while giving birth. After he recovered, he confirmed that on leaving the turret he did indeed think that the rest of us had already bailed out, and was intending to do the same, hence making his way to the exit door. He spent a long-spell in hospital, during which time his place in the crew was taken by Sergeant Rees[62].

The next day, 'Chiefy' reported the damage and our aircraft was taken off line and sent for repairs[63]. Inspecting the damage, it was soon clear that we had been hit by friendly fire. Two incendiary bombs had struck our aircraft from above, dropped by another bomber that was flying against the stream. As well as the damage to the fuselage and the mid upper turret, the port outer had also been hit, though this was the result of flak just as we started our bombing run. There was no doubt we'd had a narrow escape, not least because the incendiaries had not fallen far enough for the strikers to overcome their creep springs and fire the detonators. Then they would have ignited and we would not have survived[64].

---

[62] *Dick later returned to operations and completed his tour, being awarded the DFC in June 1944. He married a WAAF sergeant, Valeria Powell, who was serving on the station at the time. She was Mentioned in a Despatch for her work with Bomber Command. Dick died of cancer in 1973.*
[63] *Lancaster LL798 was repaired and later flown by 300 Squadron and various HCUs before being struck off charge.*
[64] *Remarkably, they were not the only squadron aircraft to be hit that night from incendiaries falling from above. The Lancaster of Flying Officer Frank Welford, a New Zealander, was also struck, causing fatal injuries to his flight engineer, Sergeant Holmes, and badly injuring the pilot and two gunners. They landed at the emergency airfield at Woodbridge. Welford later went on to be awarded the DFC.*

Names such as Venissieux (in eastern France), Rennes, Sangatte, and Aulnoye began appearing in my log book as we attacked motor and munition works, marshalling yards, military camps, ammunition dumps, and coastal gun batteries to support the opening of the Second Front. We also had a new Officer Commanding 626 Squadron. Philip Haynes had been promoted Group Captain, and his place taken by Wing Commander Quentin Ross, another regular air force type. Unfortunately, Ross was only with us for a few weeks before he was shot down by one of the German nightfighter 'aces' and so I remember little of his tenure[65]. He was in turn replaced by Wing Commander Rodney AFC, a good-natured Canadian who was very well liked and respected. He had a totally non-military way about him and so was popular with all[66].

As a crew, we flew three operations in May, but fortunately missed the somewhat disastrous raid on the military base at Mailly Le Camp in which a great many bombers were shot down. We lost three from our own Squadron and seven from Wickenby in all, with four other crews failing to return from 12 Squadron. It was a most unsatisfactory state of affairs[67].

---

[65] *Wing Commander Quentin Ross had joined the RAF at the end of 1931, his service number, coincidentally (32111), following that of Jeffrey Quill (32110), the famous Spitfire test pilot. Ross was shot down on the infamous 'Night of the Strong Winds' (24 March, 1944), the last major attack on Berlin during the Battle that bore its name. He was flying with a crew whose regular skipper, Fred Bladon, had just been promoted. Ross' aircraft was stalked and downed by Heinz-Wolfgang Schnaufer, the Night Ghost of St Trond, for Schnaufer's 50th kill. Also lost that night was the crew of Flight Sergeant Keith Margetts, who'd flown his first 'Second Dickey' with Humphrey's crew. Margetts had survived a scare on one of his first operations as captain, when his aircraft was shot at by another Lancaster! Two engines were set on fire, and substantial damage inflicted on the bomb bay and rear turret.*

[66] *Wing Commander George Rodney, who was born in Calgary, had earned his Air Force Cross before the war, helping to train new pilots on the Wellington while 'A' Flight Commander of 148 Squadron. By 1941 he'd been promoted Squadron Leader, but a pause in further promotions resulted from a period of unintended leave, having been shot down and interned in Spain for a year.*

[67] *The three crews were: Flight Sergeant Percy Barkway RCAF; Pilot Officer David Jackson DFC; and Pilot Officer Norman Fisher. There were no survivors from any of the three aircraft. Mailly Le Camp was an assembly point for German troops and armour as well as the Divisional HQ for the 21st Panzer Regiment. Although the raid was well planned, delays in the marking and a breakdown in communication between those controlling the attack obliged the Main Force to circle and the nightfighters to gather. The result was slaughter, with 42 Lancasters shot down out of the 330 that reached the target area. Some 255 Bomber Command aircrew were killed in a single night.*

We closed the month with an attack on Duisberg in the west of the Ruhr (and home to Germany's largest inland port). Our skipper described the raid as 'a fiasco' at least in the early stages, with bombs dropping 'quite blindly'. Others struggled to find the target. It was a wonder there were no more collisions or incidents of friendly fire[68].

With the invasion of Europe now imminent, the frequency of operations increased significantly in that early summer, and on June 6th – D-Day – we put on a full Squadron show with 19 Lancasters and crews all heading out to attack Acheres to the north east of Paris and a large number of us being obliged to abandon our attack on the instructions of the Master Bomber. Although it was somewhat of an anti-climax, we did marvel at the sight of the huge armada of ships of all sizes making their way across the Channel to Normandy, and knew then, that the Germans were in for a Titanic struggle.

My logbook for June records six operations (five with Neilson and the sixth with Group Captain Haynes), including two that are entered in green ink to denote a daylight attack. We were now in yet another phase of the bombing war, lending tactical support to the army, and preventing German reinforcements from reaching the front line. The Germans for a long time had believed that the invasion could only come from one direction, the Pas de Calais, and to maintain the deception, we had been obliged to bomb targets in the vicinity to keep them guessing. Now that the cat was out of the proverbial bag, we could focus all of our attentions on the 'real' targets, and that also meant operating in daylight.

Being a night bombing force, this was totally alien to us. At night, you felt safe. Of course, there was always the invisible menace, but what you couldn't see didn't scare you, and I was not much one for imagining things. We knew there were fighters; we knew there was flak, but flying at night left you in blissful ignorance of the dangers outside, and of the destruction you were causing below. Even when we did see one of our own aircraft under attack, or exploding, it somehow didn't seem quite real. You could convince yourself it might not have been one of yours after all.

---

[68] *The crew flew with a second dickey that night (21 May) – Flying Officer William Foote – who went on to win the Distinguished Service Order (DS0), and his mid upper gunner the DFM, for fighting off a determined night fighter attack and still completing their operation. At one point their aircraft was on fire.*

At HCU, three of us had been trained to fly in formation. It was for a 'Wings for Victory' Appeal, if I recall, and the Mayor of Sheffield was giving a speech. We had been asked to provide a flypast, and so at the allotted time the three of us roared past, pretty much at zero feet. It was an especially cloudy day, and as we all emerged from the gloom I can only imagine the shocked looks on the faces of the crowd below. It must have been quite terrifying. It was also rather exhausting for the flight engineer, having to synchronise the engines and maintain a constant power and speed to stay in formation.

Happily, in daylight, the formations we flew would best be described as 'loose'. Unlike our American friends whose formation flying was something to behold, we looked rather more bedraggled. Even so, seeing so many aircraft in the air at any one time was still a daunting sight, and you had a keep a close eye on what was going on around you. Watching one of your aircraft being shot down, and falling from the sky from 15,000ft and being unable to do anything about it, was both terrifying and unnerving. Confidence could quickly evaporate.

Eric Simms, our bomb aimer, probably had the best view, and in his autobiography, he writes eloquently about what he could see as the green fields flickered beneath him. For my part, daylights often meant flying relatively short trips to Northern France, and attacking at a comparatively low level, certainly low enough such that you could pick out movement on the ground and could quite clearly see your bombs exploding. It was also low enough to bring you into range of German light flak, which could be deadly.

There was also another change related to our operations so close to the front line, and that was that we were issued with a personal side-arm and five rounds. The idea was that if we were shot down we might have to shoot our way out of trouble, and were given instruction on the range accordingly. The first problem for me was a practical one: where did you put it? Some people tucked them into the top of their boot, but that was uncomfortable, particularly during a long flight, and if you baled out there was the chance your boots would fall off. The second issue was whether I really thought I was capable of a gunfight with the Germans. I decided on reflection never to carry the weapon, and I can't recall many who did, though I do remember a handful who carried knives.

Indeed, the whole fear now of being shot down was brought into sharp reflection. It had often occupied my thoughts. We were issued with an escape kit with basic rations, a compass, money, a silk map of Northern Europe etc, and others used to go prepared with a knife. I worried first about bailing out and losing my boots, and then about what I'd do as soon as I hit the ground. You tried to form a clear picture in your mind. Where would I bury my 'chute? Was I the only one who made it out alive? Would they already be out looking for me? Did I risk approaching the first civilian I came across? This was always assuming, of course, that I'd come down in 'friendly' territory, and not over one of the big cities that I'd just bombed. We'd already heard stories of our boys being lynched by angry mobs, as Londoner's had beaten up Luftwaffe crews shot down during the Blitz.

Former evaders had given lectures on escape and evasion, and by 1943/44 there were well-established evasion lines of loyal French, Belgians and Dutch who would hide you and lead you to safety. But how did you know who was loyal, or who could betray you? There was also the issue of my religion. Although when I'd started out in the RAF my dog tags proclaimed my Jewish heritage, before operating these had been exchanged for ones that said 'C of E'. I had no intention of advertising I was a Jew! It was perhaps fortunate that I was never tested, for I'm never quite sure what would have happened if I'd found myself in the hands of the Gestapo.

Humphrey's original dog tag betrayed his Jewish faith. On ops he swapped them so that they proclaimed his faith to be 'C of E'. Discretion was, he felt, by far the better part of valour under the circumstances.

On 14 June, we bombed the docks and harbour facilities at Le Havre. We were there and back in under four hours, and did considerable damage to the German Navy's fast torpedo boat (E-Boat) community. We had an escort of Spitfires, which was most unusual, but a welcome sight, and just before our bombing run (we were part of the first wave), specially-adapted Lancaster from 617 Squadron dropped their purpose-built 'Tallboy' bombs to open the attack. There was much chatter at the post-op debriefing about the extent of the damage we'd caused, and general consensus that we'd done a good job.

Harris was at this stage still experimenting a little with us and on our return from Aulnoye, with Group Captain Haynes in command, one of the gunners spotted a small aircraft approaching from the rear, and rapidly overtaking us. It appeared, he said to be belching red flame from its engine. This was one of the first of the 'V' weapons then being launched against England from dozens of permanent and temporary sites (known as 'No Ball' sites) that began springing up all over Northern France. Thus, we had a new target, and wasted a thoroughly disproportionate number of bombs (not to mention aircraft and lives) in trying to hit them.

A more satisfying target was the stronghold of Caen. The capture of Caen had actually been an objective of the first day of the invasion but now, several weeks after the event, it remained resolutely in German hands. Our troops and theirs had become pinned down, and were fighting a war of attrition. A decisive blow was needed, and so the commanders called in the Bomber boys to make the difference.

The instructions had actually come from 21st Army Group headquarters and on 7 July, we flew low over the Normandy beachhead on the run up to the target, on the northern outskirts of the city. It was, I recall, a clear summer's evening and the air was full of our aircraft, inching their way to the target, all desperate to avoid the puffs of black smoke that warned us of flak up ahead.

Eric was in the nose, giving us a running commentary of what he could see in front of him. He was transfixed by two aircraft in particular that seemed to be edging closer and closer to one another, on a line of deadly convergence. The inevitable happened and the pair collided, pieces of engine cowling and wreckage flying past us or striking the leading edges of our wings. It was a sad and desperate sight. Eric continued his commentary as one aircraft steadily lost height and disappeared below us while the other flew on. We were only at 7,000ft and neither aircraft had much margin to play with.

Our own attack was rather more successful, and we achieved a good concentration of bombs, even though there was quite a bit of flak flying all over the place. It was a grand finale for Johnny Neilson, for this was his last trip of his second tour, and he was screened[69].

We went back to Caen in the early morning of 18 July (we had originally been detailed to fly the evening before) as a prelude to the new 'Goodwood'

---

[69] *Although not an exact science, a first tour in Bomber Command typically comprised 30 operations, and the second, 20. Aircrew could not be obliged to fly a third, but many did.*

offensive, this time with Haynes at the controls, and inflicted further damage. On this occasion, there were almost 1,000 of us in the air at any one time – a most spectacular sight, jinking around in the clear air – and with the sheer weight of bombs falling, it was difficult to see how anyone could survive the holocaust we were creating below us. We were home in time for breakfast and a congratulatory message from the British commander!.

Sandwiched in-between these two raids I flew with a different pilot. His name was Pilot Officer Ronald Lone, and it was obvious that his nerves were shot. He had the jitters and I'm not surprised, because only a few weeks earlier he had survived a murderous attack over Aulnoye in which he had been wounded. I was surprised, given the extent of his injuries, that he had been returned to operations so quickly as he was clearly not well. Fortunately, the operation, a low-level attack on the railway yards and sidings at Tours, passed without incident, but I was in no rush to fly with him again[70].

My tour ended with that second operation to Caen with the Group Captain. It was my 29th and, it was decided, my last. It brought my total flying hours to almost 500, more than 200 of which had been at night. At the end of every month our logbooks had to be certified as correct by our flight commander and the Officer Commanding, and in mine, Wing Commander Rodney added 'Good show, best of luck' – very much in keeping with the language of the time.

It is difficult to convey exactly how I felt. We all shook hands upon landing, but other than that there was silence as we contemplated what had been and what was yet to come. There was certainly a sense of relief. I had been perpetually scared, although being scared had become the new 'norm' and I'd learned to live with it.

---

[70] *The citation for Lone's DFC reads: 'This officer has completed many sorties, including seven attacks on Berlin. He has displayed notable skill and set a fine example in pressing home his attacks. On a recent occasion he successfully bombed the railway junction at Aulnoye. On the homeward flight the aircraft was struck by anti-aircraft fire and Pilot Officer Lone sustained multiple wounds. In spite of his injuries, this gallant pilot insisted in remaining at the controls whilst another member of the crew attended to his injuries as much as possible. Although in great pain and much weakened by the loss of blood Pilot Officer Lone succeeded in reaching an airfield where he landed the aircraft safely. This officer displayed high qualities of skill, courage and endurance and his example was beyond praise.' Happily, Lone survived the war.*

DISTINCTIONS FOR AIRMEN

D.F.C. and D.F.M.s

Three Jewish airmen whose names appear in an Air Ministry list of awards, issued last week, are Acting Flight Lieutenant Humphrey Bernard Phillips, R.A.F.V.R., No. 626 Squadron, who receives the Distinguished Flying Cross, and Flight Sergeant Abraham Garcia, R.A.F.V.R., No. 76 Squadron, and Flight Sergeant Michael Julius Gibbons, R.A.F.V.R., No. 138 Squadron, each of whom receives the Distinguished Flying Medal. The awards have been made in recognition of gallantry and devotion to duty in the execution of air operations, the airmen, in the words of the citation, having "completed many successful operations, during which they have displayed high skill, fortitude, and devotion to duty."

F/LT. H. PHILLIPS

For Flt. Lt. Phillips this is his second honour, as he was mentioned in dispatches in January this year. He is the son of Mr. and Mrs. Samuel Phillips, of 3, Claremont Drive, Headingly, Leeds, and formerly of Phillimore Gardens, London, N.W.10, and a grandson of the late Humphrey J. Phillips, who was the well-known Secretary and Beadle of the New West End Synagogue. He was

F/SGT. A. GARCIA   F/SGT. M. GIBBONS

born in 1920 in London and was educated at Kent Coast College, Herne Bay. Enlisting in 1940, he was commissioned in 1943. A sister, Eileen, is a Sergeant in the A.T.S.

Flt. Sgt. Garcia, who is an air gunner, is the son of Mr. J. Garcia, of 35, Florence Avenue, Morden, Surrey, and he was born in Hackney in 1924. Before the war he was a compositor. He was educated at Crawford Street School, Camberwell. He has completed over 30 flights over enemy territory, five of them over Germany.

Flt. Sgt. Gibbons, who is 20, is the son of Mr. and Mrs. W. Gibbons, of 33, Thanet Lodge, Mapesbury Road, London, N.W. He studied at the Regent Street Polytechnic and was in the A.T.C.

The award of Humphrey's DFC is announced in the Jewish Chronicle.

I'd been blessed with three tremendous skippers in Haynes, Neilson and Spiller. I had only once had reason to disagree with any of their actions, and that had been with Johnny. Mid-way through our tour we had been outbound, over the North Sea, when Paddy had come on the intercom to say that his turret was u/s. It was jammed on the beam, and try as he may he couldn't move it. The skipper asked me to go aft and see if there was anything I could do but there wasn't. There was no obvious sign of anything obstructing the turret's movement, and there were no signs of any oil or hydraulic leaks (it was a Frazer Nash turret and so hydraulically powered). Everything seemed to be in working order, only it wasn't, and so I returned to my station to make my report.

Neilson told Paddy that we'd be carrying on, and instructed the mid upper gunner to watch the area of sky that the rear gunner could no longer cover. In my view, this was incredibly dangerous. It left us with only one, fully effective gunner and another who could only shoot up or down! It was also dangerous for Paddy; if we'd been hit, he would not have been able to rotate his turret to get back into the fuselage to retrieve his parachute pack, and that seemed doubly irresponsible. I felt most uncomfortable but kept my counsel. As it happened, later on into the flight the turret appeared to free itself and there was no harm done. Perhaps Johnny had been right all along; it certainly reflected his 'press on' spirit.

For a few brief days, I was in a state of limbo, and had pause to reflect on how lucky I had been. The Squadron had been a happy one, and our morale had always held, despite the losses we suffered. From November 1943 to the end of my tour in July 1944, we lost more than 150 men killed in action. Only a handful of those shot down managed to evade or attain the comparative safety of a prisoner of war camp. It was a sobering thought, though other squadrons suffered much greater losses.

As for medals, we were all recognised in some way or another with the exception of Paddy, which I always found terribly unfair. He had shared the same risks as us all, and I can only imagine that his nationality counted again him[71]. For my own part I was awarded the Distinguished Flying Cross, the citation confirming that I had '...completed many successful operations...' during which I had apparently '...displayed high skill, fortitude, and devotion to duty.' The award was published in one of the September issues of The London Gazette, and shortly afterwards an article appeared in a local Jewish newspaper where I was 'celebrated' along with two other Jewish airmen, Flight Sergeant Abraham Garcia of 76 Squadron and Flight Sergeant Michael Gibbons of 138 Squadron, both receiving the DFM.

Of the crew, we loitered at Wickenby for a few more days while they worked out what to do with us. In early August, we were posted to various training establishments to begin our period of 'rest' before perhaps being called back for a further tour, potentially against the Japanese. In my case, I was ordered to report to 1668 Heavy Conversion Unit, very much returning to my roots as Flight Engineer Leader[72].

---

[71] *Paddy was commissioned and survived the war.*
[72] *The 626 Squadron Operations Record Book shows that Eric Simms was posted to 1667 CU, Bob Bond was posted to 86 OTU, and Bill Freeman sent to 18 OTU.*

Chapter Eight – Back to School

By the Autumn of 1944 it was clear that it was no longer a case of *if* we would win the war, but rather when, and whether we could have it all wrapped up by Christmas. The assault on Germany from the air continued with breath-taking power and efficiency, and Bomber Command was still in need of fully-trained crews. The German night fighters did not know when they were beaten.

I enjoyed a week's leave before reporting for my new posting at RAF Bottesford in Rutland. Bottesford had been a US Air Force base and only just handed back by the Americans to their British counterparts. Unfortunately, they had left it in a very poor state of repair, and it would be many weeks before the situation was properly sorted. It all left something of a sour taste, and there were quite a few visits in those first few days from senior officers from both the RAF and USAAF to inspect the damage and decide what was to be done. Repairs were hampered by a shortage of tools and equipment. Luckily, my billet was one of the few that was still in one piece, and so I was not particularly affected.

I was one of the first of the instructors to arrive and reported to the station commander, Group Captain Charles Flinn, a kindly man who had been a pilot in the Royal Flying Corps. I learned that the Chief Flying Instructor was Wing Commander Brian Hallows DFC, known as 'Darkie' because of his luxurious black hair and moustaches, and that the Engineering Officer was Wing Commander William King, by all accounts a most efficient officer. Within days we were joined by another chief flying instructor, Squadron Leader John Shorthouse DFC, so that we now had a Chief Flying Instructor for each Flight[73].

---

[73] *Group Captain Flinn had been Mentioned in Despatches as a young flying officer for action over Somaliland in 1920. Wing Commander Hallows was also a regular air force officer who had taken part in the famous daylight attack on the M.A.N factory at Augsburg in 1942 in which seven of the 12 raiders were shot down and the raid leader, Squadron Leader John Nettleton, had been awarded the Victoria Cross. Squadron Leader Shorthouse was one of three New Zealand brothers to serve in the second world war. He had an eventful war, including being shot down and badly burned in 1940 and serving with a Photo Reconnaissance (PR) unit during the Battle of Britain. After a period instructing overseas, he served with 44 (Rhodesia) Squadron in 1943/44 before becoming CFI at 5 LFS and subsequently CFI at 1668 on 19 August, 1944. He later formed and commanded 189 Squadron at RAF Bardney.*

I was delighted also to discover that the Chief Ground Instructor was none other than Squadron Leader Barnes, who I had not seen since my days at Lindholme, and who had been a tower of strength. I never did discover what Barnes had been in 'civvie' street, but he was a most effective RAF officer, extremely good at his job, and with an ability to get things done[74]. We teamed up again straight away, and were soon foraging in the local area for eggs, poultry and Game from the local farms (and the local farmer's daughter – a strange girl with 'mad' eyes) to supplement the rather banal provisions in the mess.

Being a new unit, we had the task of setting everything up from scratch, and that meant once again scrounging various parts of aircraft fuselage and systems to use for ground instruction. Once again in this respect I was lucky; neighbouring RAF Station Woolfox Lodge had a complete fuel system going spare and I helped myself to it. The other respective 'leaders' had similar challenges, especially the gunnery leader, as turrets were in short supply![75]

Something that we soon had plenty of, however, was aircraft. As well as the Merlin-powered Lancaster I and IIIs, we also had 18 Lancaster IIs, equipped with Hercules VI and XV engines. This was something of a mixed blessing; we not only had the Merlin XXs and XXIIs that were 'genuine' Rolls Royce engines, but also the XXVIIIs and XXXVIIIs that had been built under license by Packard with the different carburettors that I have mentioned previously.

---

[74] *Colin Barnes was a Volunteer Reserve pilot, commissioned on 29 January 1941. On operations with 12 Squadron, he'd had his fair share of scrapes, including a serious accident on the evening of 6 February 1942 on a return from Brest. He'd been obliged to abandon his attack and was heading for home when his Wellington crashed in bad weather, with the bombs still on board. All of the crew sustained injuries, and Barnes was seriously hurt. He recovered, however, to complete his tour and be awarded the DFC, Gazetted on 13 March 1942 for his handling of a damaged aircraft and returning it to the UK. The citation for this award states: "This officer has carried out sorties over heavily-defended targets, including Berlin, Stettin, Wilhelmshaven, Hamburg and Cherbourg. His attacks have been carried through with skill and determination and on numerous occasions he has remained in heavy-defence concentrations while making several runs over the target. He is a fine operational pilot and captain of aircraft." Barnes never returned to operational flying and became an instructor, being Mentioned in Despatches in June 1944, June 1945 and then again in the New Years' Honours in January 1946. Records from the London Gazette show that Barnes was still a serving officer in 1957.*
[75] *One of the more interesting characters among the support staff was the Base accountant officer, Wing Commander Edwin Saunders MBE MM. Saunders had served in the Hertfordshire Regiment in the first world war and won the Military Medal as a Lance Corporal for conspicuous gallantry in the Battle of the Ancre Heights, part of the Battle of the Somme. He was later commissioned within the Middlesex Regiment.*

For new flight engineers under instruction, this was quite a bit to take in, for they had to know the different performance criteria of each engine, how much fuel they consumed, at what rate, what maximum boost could be attained etc. For my part, I kept a note in a little black book that I took with me when flying. It had such crucial information as the maximum time 'through the gate' (ie on maximum power which was typically three minutes) and maximum time on climbing power (for example 3,000 rpm and whatever you could get out of the supercharger. You looked for +12 boost but that could depend on what height you were flying. The higher you went, the thinner the air, and the less power you could get).

For the maintenance ground crews, the multiple engine types and variants were also a problem. They too had to learn the differences in how the engines were constructed, and specialist tools were in short supply. It was remarkable that they achieved the operational efficiency that they did, and they were always very anxious to keep us happy and in the air.

With the tools at our disposal, the instructors put together a flying training syllabus and a 35-day course that would comprise approximately 40 hours of flying (20 hours by day and 20 by night) divided across the two 'marks', with the Lancaster IIs only being used for daytime duals and solos. The authorities wanted crews to go to their squadrons trained at night on the type they would be flying on operations.

Flying training was divided into a series of Exercises of varying lengths and complexity, designed to test the skills of the individual aircrew categories as well as the performance of the crew as a whole. Exercise one, for example, included dual training on taxying, take-off, climb, and both medium and steep turns. It similarly included three-engine flying, stalling, and a controlled rate of descent to simulate an approach to landing. It lasted two hours, and required the close observation of a staff pilot and flight engineer. Exercise 18, the last Exercise on which the crews were assessed, involved a five and a half hour 'Bullseye' with the co-operation of fighter and searchlight defences, and the dropping of two bombs on a dedicated range. (We used two ranges for bombing practice at Ragdale and Wardley.) It was as close to the 'real' thing as we could replicate in a training environment.

My team of flight engineer instructors was kept fully employed both in the air and on the ground, for the first week of any new crew's training was given over to ground instruction. Every exercise was preceded by a detailed, early morning briefing in which we often took part, especially when it involved

Not all Lancs had Merlins. 1668 ground crews had the task of servicing multiple Lancaster types. The Lancaster II was powered by four Bristol Hercules engines. Above: a Lancaster MkII of 514 Sqn is shown on final approach. The pilot, F/O Bob Langley DFC, was the first to survive a tour of thirty ops with that particular unit (Marilyn Langley).

understanding the airframe and engines, as well as what to do in an emergency. Every crew was also obliged to spend at least one hour in the instructional fuselage to understand the differences between the three marks of Lancaster, and the pilots and flight engineers had to pay particular attention to the petrol and oil systems, as well as engine handling.

Much of our work tended to be focused on the earlier exercises, on airmanship and how to manage the Lancaster safely in the air and on the ground. There was also considerable emphasis placed on matters of safety, with every pilot and flight engineer obliged to pass a blindfold test of drills before being allowed to fly solo. The latter exercises evolved into the more operational aspects of every flight, from fighter affiliation to bombing procedures. We were also encouraged not only to keep a close eye on our own aircrew categories, but also to monitor the performance of the other 'trades'.

We were soon ready to commence our first conversion course, and on 1 September the first 10 crews arrived from 1 Group to start the final stage of their training prior to becoming operational. While each of the crews picked themselves a flight engineer and settled in, we continued with our practice flying, particularly on the Lancaster IIs with which only one of the pilot instructors had any experience.

My first flight on the mark was on 28 August; having earlier reported to stores for my personal flying kit (including a new type of flying boot – black shoes at the bottom and a detachable fleece lining to the top of the calf) I donned my parachute harness and Mae West for an hour of local flying with Squadron Leader Shorthouse. I flew another with Wing Commander Hallows in September. As it was, the frequency of flying was nothing as intense as it had been at 1656, and the vast majority of my time was given over to ground instruction, leaving my team of flight engineers to do their share.

As an aircrew category, flight engineers were a mixed bag, with varying degrees of education and ages. Typically, they might have had some spurious engineering background (like me there were a number that had been apprentice mechanics) but that was no indicator of intelligence, or that they were especially suited to the job. Certainly, I noticed how the quality of trainee changed over the years I spent instructing.

Very occasionally, I might be taking a class that included an experienced pilot and flight engineer (they attended lectures together) and this could be quite disruptive and distracting to others. On more than one occasion I was obliged to bring them down a peg or two, but largely this was the exception rather than the rule.

Before the beginning of a lecture, I would often use a dummy control panel to create an in-flight scenario and test the engineers on what the dials might be telling them (for example, that the port outer was just about to boil over), and what remedial action was required. Whereas some would be able to identify the problem and the resolution immediately, others took an alarmingly long time. Some never got it at all. Considering that this was on the ground, in the relative calm of a classroom, I didn't much care for their chances if it happened in the air, over Germany, with flak and fighters all around and the skipper barking at them on the intercom! It was my job to make them competent at least, but not all were technically minded, and some were quickly out of their depth.

Inevitably, the unit suffered its fair share of incidents or accidents, although it was not until December that we lost our first aircraft. A young Canadian flying officer was on a cross country exercise on 12 December when his mid upper gunner reported a fire in the port outer engine. The flight engineer correctly feathered the engine and the pilot called flying control to await instructions.

He was told to make a detour to East Kirby, as our airfield was now covered in fog.

A Lancaster flies perfectly well on three engines and the pilot, Leo Richer, was not unduly concerned, until the flight engineer informed him that the starboard outer was now playing up, and showing an alarming drop in oil pressure. Again, the Lancaster was capable of flying on two without too much difficulty, but landings could be treacherous. On reaching East Kirby, which was itself covered in a thick haze, the flight engineer fired off a red distress flare to be answered with a green and immediate permission to land. The pilot did well, right until the moment the aircraft touched the ground and he landed so heavily that he bounced 50ft back into the air and overshot.

With the two good engines screaming, the pilot managed to make height and told his crew to take up crash positions. Despite his left Oleo leg dangling loose, the pilot was able to wrestle the Lancaster into level flight and crash land in a farm field a short distance from the airfield perimeter. As the aircraft skidded to a halt it broke in two, the wings dropped off, and the aircraft burst into flames. Fortunately, all of the crew made it out in one piece to be greeted by a farmer's boy who offered them a cup of tea!

In the Court of Enquiry that followed, the presiding officer found that the error was part engine failure (to be specific it was a flame trap failure) and part pilot error. From my perspective, the flight engineer had done all that was asked of him, and the crew went on to pass their course. I flew with Richer on a night time solo a few days later and he appeared none the worse for his adventures[76].

The New Year of 1945 arrived with a new promise that the end of the war in Europe was in sight. Allied forces were now knocking at the enemy's door and defeat seemed inevitable. Our eyes were increasingly on the Far East, recognising that although the war in the west was almost over, the Japanese were as yet far from conquered.

The organisation behind our Heavy Conversion Unit changed at the end of 1944 when we became part of the newly-formed 7 Group (Training) Bomber Command based at St Vincent's, Grantham. Our own station at Bottesford was

---

[76] *Leo Richer and his crew were posted to 90 Squadron at RAF Tuddenham to fly operations in the last few weeks of the war. He survived and returned to Canada to start a water taxi business. He died in 2000.*

combined with RAF Langar to become a single administrative unit, 72 Base, and Group Captain Flinn was appointed to take command with his place in turn being taken by Group Captain Ken Batchelor DFC[77]. The Base Engineering Officer was Wing Commander Norman Wakelin[78].

Towards the end of January I was posted on a Bomber Command Instructors' Course which lasted until mid-February.

It meant I missed a rather spectacular accident on 7 February: one of our instructors, Flying Officer Walker, was with a Canadian pupil pilot practising a three-engined overshoot when they got it all horribly wrong. The Lancaster crashed 400 yards beyond the runway and burst into flames. Soon after it was learned that the pilot had been rather too keen to take the flaps up before gaining enough height, with the inevitable consequences. The pilot, pupil and one of my flight engineers were injured, the pupil badly enough to be taken to hospital[79].

Unlike the Flight Engineer Leaders' Course, the Instructors' Course was a positive experience from which I gleaned much valuable information and did rather better in my end of course exam, receiving an A2. Even then I felt that I should have done better. But that may have just been conceit. As an instructor, I felt it could so easily have been me who was taking the course, rather than being the student.

Minor incidents were plenty at 1668, and engine fires both in the air and on the ground an occupational hazard. There were also incidents of bird strikes, overheating brakes, and even an exploding H2S radar set. Aircraft getting bogged down on the soft verges was a common occurrence. They could sink so low as to damage the spinning propellers. Sometimes the crew got it wrong, like when the flight engineer brought the flaps up too early, and on other occasions it was simply bad luck. Sometimes the instructors got it wrong, the danger, perhaps, of over-confidence or complacency. We also had a number

---

[77] *Batchelor was not in the post long before being posted out to command RAF Mildenhall and Flinn resumed his position as station commander. Air Commodore John Merer arrived from Syerston to assume command of 72 Base, each Base then being commanded by an officer of Air rank. Merer, a former RFC pilot and specialist navigator, was later closely involved with directing the Berlin Airlift.*

[78] *Later Group Captain Norman Wakelin. Retired from the service on 12 August, 1966.*

[79] *Flying Officer John Walker RAFVR had been awarded his DFC while serving with 622 Squadron in the Autumn of 1944. The pupil, Flying Officer F G Wilkinson, was taken to RAF Hospital Rauceby.*

The station commander helps ground staff remove essential items from a crashed Lancaster that continues to burn.

of thoroughly avoidable accidents, such as vehicles driving into aircraft in the dark, and these were particularly frustrating.

I had my own little accident one afternoon when out on my bicycle (again!). The size of Bottesford was such that bicycles were necessary to get around the station, and some of us were lucky enough to own RAF-issue bikes, which were particularly robust. Coming around a corner at speed I ran headlong into another cyclist heading in the opposite direction. Unfortunately for him, he had his own bicycle which was rather more fragile than my own and was badly bent. On reflection, I should have helped pay for the repairs!

While I was away, flying had been greatly restricted owing to the weather. The problem had been compounded by a shortage of pilot instructors many of who, like me, had been sent away for further training. On one of the few afternoons that flying was possible, the unit suffered its first fatalities when on 15 January one of our crews crashed whilst on a training bombing exercise. The Australian captain, Pilot Officer Thompson, was killed along with most of his crew. Only the rear gunner survived. The aircraft was thoroughly burned.

While I was away, also, we had another turnaround in senior officers: Hallows was posted out, and acting Wing Commander William Crebbin DFC posted in

Learning the hard way: accidents were as commonplace at 1668 as at other HCUs.

to replace him as a Chief Flying Instructor. We similarly had a number of pilot instructors arrive to swell the ranks of our permanent staff[80].

The difficulties caused by the poor weather were two-fold: on the one hand, it meant that we fell behind in delivering our quota of crews to the front-line squadrons (most of our crews went to squadrons within 1 and 3 Groups, while those with the most promise went straight to 8 Group); on the other, it meant

---

[80] *Hallows was appointed to command 627 Squadron Pathfinder Force at Woodhall Spa. He retired as a Wing Commander OBE, DFC, AE. Crebbin, a Volunteer Reserve officer, had won his DFC with 7 Squadron in 1942 while still a Flight Lieutenant.*

Flight Engineer Instructors' Course, March 1945. Humphrey gained more from this particular course than from previous training.

that the station became somewhat overcrowded, as new courses arrived before the existing courses had time to finish and move out[81].

Efforts were made to keep everyone busy, with every kind of sport being organised for men and women alike, and the creation of an indoor sports hall to use when the snow was at its thickest. A mess party was also arranged of which I remember very little other than there being bags of booze, plenty of girls, and a rather dangerous game known as 'high cockalorum' that seemed to comprise jumping over sofas and armchairs in the form of a human steeplechase!

The only positive aspect of the poor weather was that it gave the ground crews time to catch up with routine maintenance, albeit that they had to work outside as well as in. It particularly gave the Engineering Officer an opportunity to sort out a series of niggling issues with fuel tank failures that led to a visit from

---

[81] *The target output of crews per month was 36 – an average between the winter output (28 per month) and the summer output of 44. At one point, there were around 2,000 RAF and WAAF on site. Airman of all nationalities were trained at 1668 including two Chinese captains who were allegedly nicknamed 'Press On' and 'Bang on'.*

Bomber Command HQ staff to assess the problem. He was reassured that the designers at AVRO were looking into it.

One particularly amusing incident I remember during my time at Bottesford occurred one morning when I was on my way from my billet to the station HQ. It was quite a distance and so I'd jumped in my car. I had gone past the WAAFs quarters and was quite near the road where a couple of the huts were situated. They were actually closer to the local village than the station HQ. Imagine my surprise when I came across a Lancaster, on its belly, nestling between two of the buildings and effectively hidden from view. I immediately went and found the Intelligence Officer to ask him whether there had been any crashed aircraft reported in the night. "No," he replied, "though we have lost a Lanc of our own." "Well," I replied, "I've just found it for you!"

My report caused quite a flap, and when they went to inspect the aircraft, they found that there was still a chap in it, unconscious on the rest bed. No-one, it appeared, knew he was there or had thought to check!

A remarkable incident occurred at the end of March when we found ourselves subjected to an enemy air attack. It had otherwise been a relatively quiet month. I had flown a handful of air tests with two of the instructor pilots – Squadron Leader Philip Brentnall DFC and Squadron Leader Ken Major DFC – to keep my hours up[82]. It was 20 March, and I was in the mess when there was a brief tannoy announcement to say that intruders had been reported over the UK and to ensure the blackout blinds were in place. Suddenly, and without warning, there was a terrific explosion as one and then a number of bombs were dropped by what was later identified as a Junkers 88.

The intruder was very low and could easily be picked out in the moonlight as it turned to make another attack. By this stage, we had all taken cover as the German raked the airfield with 20mm cannon before it again turned and finally sped off into the night. Intruders were a danger, and the Luftwaffe was

---

[82] *Squadron Leader Philip Brentnall DFC had been a flight commander with 218 (Gold Coast) Squadron. He arrived at Bottesford in February from No 3 Lancaster Finishing School, where he had also been a flight commander. He survived the war and flew the DH Comet on its maiden flight to Johannesburg in 1952. He later received the Queen's Commendation for Valuable Service in the Air as a 707 Captain with BOAC. Squadron Leader Kenneth Major had won his DFC with 100 Squadron in May 1944. He was posted out in April 1945 to resume flying duties with 83 Squadron. He died in 2017.*

undoubtedly attempting one last 'hurrah!' before finally admitting defeat, and we were lucky that there weren't any casualties either on the ground or from any aircraft in the circuit. Indeed, only one of our Lancasters (JW252) was reported as 'damaged', which was a pretty poor return for the effort made by the German pilot[83].

Marshal of the Royal Air Force Lord Trenchard, the father of the RAF, came to visit us in April, one of several senior officers doing the rounds. It reminded me of an earlier visit by another senior officer, Sir Philip Joubert de la Ferté, who was for a time the AOC-in-C Coastal Command and later Inspector General of the RAF. We'd of course been expecting him, and the mess had been laid out with a top table, rather like a wedding. The Station Commander went to show Sir Philip to his seat but he declined, and insisted instead that he sat with the more junior officers on the other tables. Thus it was I found myself sitting in close proximity to this rather grand gentlemen, who impressed us with his knowledge of our unit, and the challenges we faced. He was a kind, friendly man who had clearly made it his business to understand who we were and what we did[84].

Victory in Europe came at the beginning of May, and the unit was stood down for 48-hours of celebration. While there was time to pause and reflect, we still had a role to play in training crews to finish off the Japanese in the Far East. And there were still dangers, as illustrated by a bizarre incident long ago forgotten but remembered in the RAF Station Bottesford records. On 26 May, one of our aircraft landed with a large hole in the mid upper turret and with the mid upper gunner slightly injured. A smoke puff had been fired and blown straight back down the fuselage, entering the turret. The pilot was lucky to get down in one piece[85].

---

[83] *Bottesford thus had the distinction of suffering the very last German bombing raid of the war against Britain.*

[84] *Air Chief Marshal Sir Philip Joubert de la Ferté KCB, CMG, DSO was an early Royal Flying Corps pilot who flew one of the first operational sorties of the war. By the end of hostilities, he was a Lieutenant-Colonel and in charge of the RAF forces in Italy. Upon the outbreak of the second world war he was AOC Air Forces in India, and on its conclusion, was a senior officer within South East Asia Command. He retired in November 1945 and died 20 years later.*

[85] *Lancaster LM 340 was eventually struck off charge in October 1945 having served with 467, 405, 635 and 57 Squadrons before arriving at 1668.*

During this time, we had the pleasure of taking our loyal ground crews on what we called 'Cooks Tours' (sometimes also called 'Ruhr Tours'), to show them the devastation we had caused. On 13 June, I went as the flight engineer with Group Captain Flinn and Wing Commander Crebbin on one such 'tour', from Base to Amsterdam, Wesel, Dortmund, Duisberg, Cologne, Bonn, Aachen, Rotterdam, and then back to Bottesford. The trip was executed at very low level, and my initial reaction to the scenes below me was one of total horror at the wanton destruction. That is not to say, however, that I was in any way ashamed of what we'd done. Although war is a terrible thing, Hitler had to be stopped, and for two years Bomber Command was the only means of really fighting back, and showing our intention to defeat his evil regime.

Whilst I was still contemplating our likely involvement in the fighting out east, suddenly it was all over. The Americans dropped not one but two atomic bombs on Japan in the first two weeks of August, and the Emperor finally threw in the towel.

After VE Day, Bomber Command ground staff were treated to 'Cooks Tours' of the German cities they had helped devastate. The above photos show Cologne (left) and Hamburg (right).

Chapter Nine – A Return to Civvie Street

I had decided as far back as 1942 that I did not want to stay in the RAF after the war. It dawned on me that I was not particularly suited to service life, and was not especially keen with the responsibility that went with it. That's not to say that the thought didn't enter my mind, more that it was an easy decision to make.

I took my very last flight on 22 February, 1946, as flight engineer to Flying Officer Roach[86]. It was a standard early-morning two-hour exercise, practicing three-engine landings. My log book was signed by the Chief Flying Instructor, Squadron Leader Runciman, confirming that I had flown just short of 550 hours, almost 215 hours of which had been at night[87]. A few days later, I was officially demobbed.

As a commissioned officer with a war-substantive rank and a volunteer, I was demobbed on probation. While conscripts could return to civilian life knowing that for them the war was finally over, for me and thousands like me, it was slightly different. I was on the reserve, which meant that if the balloon went up again, I could immediately be called back for active service. I couldn't entirely relax.

The process of being demobbed was completed with alarming efficiency. I remember little of the event, other than the impressive way in which the tailor was able to estimate my size without the need of a tape measure. Thus kitted out in a new suit, hat and shoes, I stepped out into a new world of peace.

My immediate challenge was finding somewhere to live. My parents by this stage had moved back from Leeds to Willesden, and I therefore returned to the family home. The house had been badly damaged during the war and since repaired. Nothing fitted quite as it had done before.

---

[86] *Most probably Flying Officer Robert Roach DFC, arrived for instructor duties in December 1944 from 186 Squadron.*
[87] *Squadron Leader Walter Runciman, a New Zealander, would receive the Air Force Cross for his work with 1668 HCU. He had earlier flown a tour in Stirlings with 7 Squadron and been awarded the DFM. He was repatriated in 1947 but returned to the UK shortly after to rejoin the RAF. In 1950 he qualified as a test pilot and was posted to Boscombe Down. Seconded to the aircraft manufacturer, Shorts, he flew the prototype SA.4 Sperrin and the SB.6 Seamew. On 9 June, 1956, he was killed while at the control of a Seamew at a flying display in Belfast.*

Returning to civilian life I turned my thoughts to my future career. I saw myself owning a repair garage in the motor trade, but without capital it remained a pipe dream. My last job had been as an 'improver' and I was almost fully trained. I'd also learned a range of additional skills in the RAF that were eminently transferrable, so I was confident I'd find something suitable. My previous employer had given me a reference and a good one, and although the firm I'd worked for before the war had long-since closed down I was still in touch with the old foreman who had gone on to set up his own business. He invited me to join him, but one look at his operation and it soon became clear that it would never work out. He'd set up his business from home, with vehicles parked on the surrounding streets and his tools scattered all over the place. It was little short of chaos, so I thanked him for the offer and we went our separate ways.

Through the grapevine, I heard that one of the major dealers, Car Mart, was expanding its operations with a new depot in Hendon, and was actively recruiting. I was interviewed and offered a job, and started work soon after. I was, it appeared, just the sort of chap they were looking for and I was pleased to be once more gainfully employed. The premises were vast and had been taken over by the Ministry of Food during the war, and the firm was doing well. It had won the agency for Austin Morris, but despite promising signs, trade was slow and I found the work incredibly boring. After about six months I was offered a promotion to Receptionist, and although the work was more interesting, and my earnings increased, it was still a long way from where I wanted to be.

At about the same time, and as part of my re-integration into a peacetime way of life, I decided to join a tennis club. I was not especially gifted as a tennis player but my motivation was twin-pronged: firstly, as a good source of exercise; and secondly, as an opportunity of broadening my social group and hopefully meeting some of the opposite sex. Despite now being in my late twenties, my experience with girls was somewhat underwhelming.

Happily, the President of the Club was a family friend and 'lent' on the captain to approve my application. Somehow, I managed to pass the 'playing in' test, despite the dubious quality of my backhand. Practice, as they say, makes perfect and steadily my tennis improved and my social circle expanded. Despite being appointed Treasurer, my success on other fronts was still limited. Things seemed to take a turn for the worse when we lost the use of our courts, and were obliged to find a new home for our club. We ended up moving from Regents Park to a new site, with a pavilion, only five minutes' walk from my home in Willesden!

Coincidentally, a problem arose over secretarial duties. We had a very nice girl in post, but her output was too low. The President proposed a replacement by the name of Iris Weber whose key attraction, he said, was that she worked for a large public company and therefore had access to a Gestetner copying machine which, in its day, was little short of revolutionary. I remonstrated that the girl was too young (she was approaching 21) but I was over-ruled. I found myself therefore compelled to make contact with this young lady, because I had a batch of papers to be copied and a map to be produced to guide members to our new venue.

I suggested to her that we met at Marble Arch, planning to walk down Park Lane and Piccadilly to a restaurant in Dover Street. It turned out to be a beautiful evening and all went well, so much so that I decided that my friend, the President, had chosen well after all. Meeting Iris proved to be the catalyst for a significant increase in the time we spent at the club, and in the amount of club business that appeared to demand our joint attention!

Our liaison did not go unnoticed, however, and inevitably one day I was summoned to the parental home to meet 'Daddy'. Suffice to say he demanded to know my intentions, and asked me a series of embarrassing questions about my income and prospects. He laughed (derisively) when he heard the miserable sum I was receiving and said simply: 'You will not keep my daughter on that!' We were told that we were to 'cool' our relationship and see something less of each other. To give you some idea of how I felt, it was like being in front of the Air Officer Commanding (AOC) and being given a dressing down. Needless to say, we both chose to ignore her father's wishes, but that I really did need to secure a better income.

Happily, my father came to the rescue. He had contacts among the senior Directors within the 600 Group, a large, well-known scrap metal merchants and machinery business, and he secured me an interview with its Road Transport Department. The present manager, they explained to me, had a heart condition and was not expected to last six months. If I did a good enough job, and my training was successful, then I could expect to be considered to take over from him in due course. The salary was not much more than I was earning anyway, but the prospects were considerably improved.

Thus I joined the firm in October 1948 as a long distance Traffic Clerk on probation, working out of its Wood Lane office. On my first day, I was told to report at 7-00am and was responsible for handing out the delivery orders to some 60 or so drivers. It was the first morning I had been up so early for a very long time, and wasn't sure I would last; in the event, I stayed with the business for almost 20 years[88].

The 600 Group had a fleet of around 1,000 vehicles, split fairly evenly between cars and commercial vehicles.

The car fleet was inclusive of 'luxury' vehicles run by the directors and belonging to the London chauffeur-driven pool. Departments paid a hire fee for the representatives' cars, based competitively against what could be obtained on the open market (the vehicles being serviced and maintained within the 'fee'). Replacement vehicles were also included as part of the scheme.

The commercial fleet comprised a range of vehicles from half ton vans up to 20-ton lorries, as well as low-loaders and other specialist vehicles. They were hired on the same basis as the cars, and split across six regional depots, each depot being run by a Transport Manager reporting to me. The remaining six (there were 12 depots in all) were run by Divisional Managers.

The commercial fleet operation was fully costed, and managers were responsible for the overall performance of their particular site. We met annually at one of the locations (the venues were rotated) to review and discuss how things were going. All of our drivers and chauffeurs were obliged to complete a RoSPA accident prevention course and we held annual awards (attended by the Directors and their wives) to recognise best performance. We also took part in nationally-organised awards such as the Lorry Driver of the Year, which we won on a regular basis.

The range of goods our vehicles carried varied enormously, from scrap iron and steel through to machine tools and cranes. The more abnormal loads tended to be the domain of the Dismantling Department, and one of the first I was involved with was the contents of the South Bank Exhibition site. A notable item was the Skylon tower, a futuristic 'vertical symbol' that was the

---

[88] *The 600 Group derived its name from its original company address, 600 Commercial Road, London. It had been founded by George Cohen & Sons at the end of the 19th Century.*

iconic feature of the Festival of Britain. It appeared to 'float' without any visible means of support, much like the British economy according to jokes at the time.

An endearing characteristic of the men within Dismantling Department was their inability to accurately estimate the weight of the goods we had to transport. On one occasion, we took an order to move an old steam crane from the Isle of Grain to Shoreditch in East London. The alleged weight was 25 tons, so we sub-contracted the job to one of our preferred hauliers with a good stock of low loaders. It was a Saturday afternoon and our long-suffering West London Garage Manager, Jim Cathcart, took a call from the contractor who was somewhat cross.

His vehicle duly loaded with the crane and travelling along an internal roadway on the Isle of Grain site, had almost turned over as the road had collapsed under its weight! A protracted salvage operation ensued, and a post mortem revealed that the crane's weight was nearer 35 than 25 tons, and therefore at least five tons too heavy for the road to cope with. It transpired that originally the crane had arrived by barge. To cap the fiasco, our haulier was using a brand-new Scammel trailer, and we had bent it!

The movement of abnormal loads on UK highways was restricted and subject to prior notification to the relevant authorities and details of the intended route. With the advent of the new motorway networks, the Ministry of Transport was particularly keen to see them being used. Such enthusiasm led to some unexpected snags.

One of our low loaders was heading north on the newly-constructed M1 and was about ten miles short of the famous Watford Gap when it developed a braking fault, obliging the driver to stop on the hard shoulder to investigate. As the vehicle slowed to a halt, the hard shoulder began to collapse under its weight, causing the lorry to turn on its side. Various frantic telephone calls followed (remembering this is well before the age of the mobile phone), and on this occasion, I went with Jim to view the scene of the crime.

The coach-built cab of the low loader was badly damaged and when we arrived the driver and his mate were removing the moveable contents to transfer to the salvage vehicle we'd brought along. There were two motorcycle police at the scene, coning off a section of the motorway.

As I watched the mate unloading the goods I noticed a large red patch on the back of his shirt and stupidly said: "What's on your shirt, John?" Lifting his shirt revealed a deep, four-inch gash above his kidney. He had been quite unaware of the injury until I'd mentioned it. After a quick consultation with one of the policeman, I drove John to the nearest Accident and Emergency department with a motorcyle escort – something of a new experience.

Abnormal loads could be abnormally long, wide or tall. The latter could be particularly troublesome, as we found once when routing a load that was sixteen feet and three inches high. The design standard was sixteen feet and six inches for all bridges, so we had three inches to spare. Alas a call arrived to say that the load had been fouled on a bridge, somewhere north of Luton. The MoT told us not to be so silly, and that all bridges were of standard height. When they measured it afterwards, however, they were obliged to concede that its height was several inches below the minimum. It appeared that it had somehow subsided in the years since it was built.

The transport affairs within the 600 Group were divided into three separate business units, with three, separate 'heads': Road; Rail and Air; and Shipping. The individuals running these units were experts in their field, and everything was smooth and efficient. Until, that is, the arrival of a new Managing Director, Jack Wellings.

Wellings was an outsider. On the retirement of the old Managing Director, Lewis Levy, the owners had looked beyond the family for a replacement. Wellings had been in charge of a smelting business in Canada, and was no doubt technically well-suited to the role. It didn't take me long, however, to conclude that Wellings had a very different management style to that of the kindly Mr Levy, and my opinion was not improved when he decided to bring in consultants to review the operational performance and efficiency of certain teams, one of those teams being mine! The consultant given to interviewing me was a Dutchman by the name of Van Tign, whose knowledge of transport matters was clearly inadequate for the task for which he'd been chosen.

The upshot of his review was that I should be promoted, and my team restructured and ultimately dismantled. I was to be responsible for taking over the three business units, with the unit heads reporting to me as Group Transport Manager. Among my first actions was to visit Foyles bookshop, to read up on the subject of shipping, and the technicalities of such things as charter parties and demurrage. I could never be as knowledgeable as those in my team, but I owed it to them to learn as much as I could.

Twelve months into my new role, with a bigger hat but no more money, I'd had enough. Several arguments with the Managing Director followed. Unbeknownst to me, my salary had been frozen for an indefinite period. I'd received no bonus, and no advance in my living allowances, despite a role that took me all over the country. The culture of the business began to change for the worse. My direct line manager was changed; previously I reported to the Head of Personnel and Transport, an international Bridge player outside of work with a phenomenal memory but little commercial sense. Now I was to report to a much younger man who was in charge of Publicity, a bumptious, unpleasant fellow with little or no manners. While Lewis Levy and the Chairman, Cyril Cohen, had both been gentlemen, this new man was everything but, and our dislike for each other was wholly mutual.

He particularly disliked my engagement with our trade body, the Freight Transport Association (FTA), considering it a total waste of time. I found it completely the opposite; by then I was serving on various Technical Committees, and found the networking and sharing of experiences and knowledge with colleagues from major corporates such as Shell and Metal Box to be especially useful. We also helped to influence the MoT's thinking on new legislation.

I had written a Paper on some proposed new regulations on plating and licensing on behalf of the FTA, and it had stirred considerable interest, not least from the publishers of our trade magazine, Commercial Motor. I was invited on an all-expenses paid press trip to the US, subject to the approval of my boss. He refused, presumably out of pure spite, but it was a sign of how far the culture of the business had declined.

I took the manner in which I was being treated as an insult, and I regarded the piecemeal deconstruction of the Road Transport Department as a tragedy. Inevitably, having consulted a solicitor, I handed in my notice. Even that included an element of farce. Wellings asked if I would be willing to be sacked, rather than resign, because in that way my pension would be protected and I'd be entitled to some severance pay. In the end, it was a relief.

For most of my time at the 600 Group I'd been treated with nothing but kindness and respect. I had been fairly treated and even occasionally given a pat on the back from the Chairman. It was only in the latter stages that my experience changed, and the fault lay directly at the feet of the new MD and his philosophy[89].

I left without a job to go to, but was not out of work for long. One of the haulage industry's more colourful characters heard that I was out of work and offered me a job. He owned his own haulage business and had been subcontracted to the 600 Group on a number of occasions so our paths had crossed. He needed a new Fleet Engineer and it was on that understanding that I agreed to join. We met, negotiated a remuneration package that we were both happy with, and drew up a contract accordingly.

Word got around quite quickly and with some surprise I took a call from my old and respected friend Hugh Featherstone, the Director General of the FTA, who asked me if I knew what I was doing. My new employer, it appeared, was inclined to sail a little close to the wind, and Hugh feared for my reputation. It was too late to back out, so I promised to be careful![90]

Within a matter of days of joining my new outfit, it was clear that Hugh's concerns were not without foundation. First off, I was not only to be the Fleet Engineer but also the Training Officer. Happily, it was a role that I could readily fulfil, but the task had never been discussed, and the additional responsibility required quite a bit of additional work. It also required setting up a more formal training regime for his drivers, of which there were more than 150.

Until then, the owner had been conducting the training himself, such as it was, for which he was entitled to an annual grant from the Road Transport Training Board (one of the quangos set up by the Labour Government of the Period) of £2,000. I felt that I could at least bring some legitimacy to the company's training claims![91]

The business was primarily involved in heavy haulage from two London bases; it also had a warehousing business with a delivery fleet in West London. The

---

[89] *Sir Jack Wellings CBE died in 2010.*
[90] *Hugh Featherstone CBE retired from the FTA in 1984. He had joined the Traders Road Transport Association, the forerunner to the FTA, in 1958. During his tenure, road hauliers became obliged to have their hours monitored by a tachograph, and subscribe to more rigorous vehicle testing. He died in 2009.*
[91] *The owner had been one of the Kinder Transport boys, an organised effort to save several thousands of Jewish children before the outbreak of the second world war. Britain alone took in some 10,000 children.*

owner's immediate concern was to complete the testing and plating of his vehicles; I had only recently overseen the transition of the 600 Group's fleet through this process (albeit with the full support of Jim Cathcart), and my boss naturally had high expectations that I could achieve the same for his team. He was somewhat surprised that I didn't appear to know the local MoT inspector personally, and encouraged me to wine and dine him, and cultivate his friendship. I did no such thing.

One morning, early in my tenure, I was presented with a pile of papers that I was asked to sign. When I enquired what they were, I'm not sure I wanted to know the answer. Needless to say, I refused to sign them unless and until the drivers had completed their necessary training, and the vehicles had been properly tested. I had no intention of being corrupt or corrupted!

I thus implemented a new training and testing regime, setting up two lorry driver training schools (one in Hornchurch and the other in Watford) and a formal schedule of maintenance and repair for the vehicles. The driver training schools were not only for our own drivers, though in selling our services to a wider audience we did little more than break even.

It would be wrong to suggest that the repair and maintenance of the owner's fleet had been totally neglected prior to my arrival, but there was certainly the occasional incident that gave cause for alarm. One in particular I recall involved the inspection of a winch on the back of a lorry whose base should have been secured by six bolts. This one only had three, which was incredibly dangerous. The winch could have easily been wrenched from its base with any particularly heavy load.

I spent the better part of seven years with the business helping to raise standards in health, safety and compliance, until my boss decided to pull the plug on his training services and therefore was in no further need of a training manager. We parted on very friendly terms, but by now I was 55 and finding another job was going to be difficult and I was too young to retire. To be more precise, I did not have enough money in my pension pot to retire, even if I wanted to.

I had enjoyed my training role and decided to apply to our industry's training board to see if there were any suitable vacancies. I also applied to the Man-made Fibre Producing Industry Training Board (MMFBITB), somewhat tongue in cheek, as I had no understanding of their industry or their products.

I fully expected my CV to be discarded at once, but by some miracle I was called for interview.

The interview, as it happens, went rather well, and they said I would hear from them. I thought they were being polite, and could not resist asking whether I had any chance at all, given my background and total ignorance of the fibres producing industry. The interview panel comprised representatives from some of the biggest organisations of the day, including ICI, Courtaulds, and Monsanto, and they all laughed. I was told that my ignorance was one of my strengths: it meant that if visiting one of their installations, I would have no idea of a secret, even if I were looking at it, and as such could not disclose anything of value (either deliberately or otherwise) even if I'd wanted to!

Coincidentally, The Road Transport Industry Training Board was the one to come back to me first with an offer where the benefits were sufficiently attractive to accept. The work was well within my comfort zone and sphere of knowledge, and the job was within walking distance of home. I was not required to start for several weeks, and in the intervening period, the MMFPITB made contact to say that I'd been successful in my application and when could I start? I explained that I had already accepted another role, and was due to start the following week, but they told me to think about it over the weekend. I agreed to call them on Monday with an answer.

There was little to choose between the two jobs: the road transport job I could probably do in my sleep; the other role offered an opportunity of experiencing an entirely new industry, and sounded both challenging and exciting. In the end I opted for the latter, and the RTITB was not best impressed. Reporting for work in the Monday and informing them of my decision to leave, they took it with good grace, but I clearly understood never to return.

Thus I embarked on a new training career in the Fibres industry, ably managed by the ICI Fibres Division under Lord Mills and based in Harrogate. I was provided with excellent literature describing the process and an equally excellent tutor to show me the ropes. I was also introduced and invited to address a group of trainers, which I did with some trepidation, opting to stay within the confines of the training basics. My answer to the simple question, 'when did you last do a training needs analysis?' elicited a rather thin response!

Perhaps my biggest challenge was more local in character, but obstinate in terms of solution. At one location I found that, although fork lift truck drivers received sound training, the Union would not accept a 'fail' if the examiner deemed the appropriate standard had not been met. Over time they saw sense, and workers' lives were no longer put at risk. One or two other long-standing issues were also sensibly overcome.

Throughout my appointment, I ensured that my periodic reports on Depots and Works were comprehensive and pulled no punches; I was not too pushy in seeking co-operation or results. But there were occasions where our powers of persuasion were tested to the full, and my secret weapon was always the threat of adverse publicity in the press.

The job lasted seven years and only came to an end because of a change in Government policy, whereby the Quangos were dissolved and the industry invited to form its own Board. With only three years to go until State retirement age, I was not invited to join the new Voluntary Training Board, but my pension was made up to include the 'missing' period so I was not financially penalised. It had been a thoroughly enjoyable time as custodian of professional training and development, and as rewarding as any previous period in my career.

If I thought that this was the end of my working life, however, then I was mistaken. A 'phone call from an acquaintance in the Engineering Industry Training Board set me on a new path, as a technical editor for a range of City and Guilds publications. Within a matter of days of accepting the post, I joined the Dutch academic publisher Klewer, working from a subsidiary office (Stam Press) in Rickmansworth.

The books were engineering trades' training publications, compiled primarily by technical college lecturers who were teaching the subjects. It was interesting and not dissimilar to the subjects I'd been covering with the MMFPITB. The transition to my new role was comparatively painless and brought me into contact with a number of very knowledgeable and able people. Our united aim was the production of clear and unambiguous training texts.

It was not always an office-bound role. Some of the authors were based in polytechnics and technical colleges all over the UK. If and when a text was particularly difficult or complex, I would visit the authors in person to discuss. I also met regularly with the City and Guilds officer responsible for the project, so in terms of meeting people, and further expanding my technical knowledge, it way a pleasant was of seeing out my career. The additional salary was also welcome.

I retired in the summer of 1985 at the same time that my wife, Iris, left her employment with the Institute of Cost and Management Accountants, where she had been employed first as a clerk and then the manager in their examinations department. The job was highly pressurised and Iris had the talent and temperament to cope with it.

Iris was of course the girl I'd met some 35 years earlier at the tennis club, the girl whose father had not originally thought me much of a catch! He had made it clear to us that since we had been seeing so much of one another, we had better get engaged. We were secretly delighted. Alas the decision did not result in the joyous spread of news we'd hoped for or expected.

During a get-together of Aunts to plan our engagement party, Iris' mother, Leah, suffered a heart attack, collapsed and died. The suddenness of her death hit her daughters and Sam, my prospective father in law, with tremendous force. My family too became involved and the gloom extended for several months.

Iris' mother had been the epitome of kindness, greatly respected and loved by all who knew her. I could not but help feeling guilty at her passing; the way I saw it, had I not met Iris and asked her to marry me, then none of this would have happened. Incidentally, my father provided me with tremendous support throughout the difficult weeks that followed.

In the event, we spent almost a whole year planning, and the wedding was finally fixed for 5 October, 1949. The ceremony was at the New West End Synagogue in Baywater, and was followed by a party at Gunters in Park Lane and a honeymoon in Torquay.

On the day of the actual wedding, I experienced a feeling of great elation never previously enjoyed, but was understandably nervous. My anxiety was not helped by the fact that Iris was late, very late. The cars went to the wrong Ridgeway, and the wedding party were obliged to abandon their vehicles for smaller cars, with only limited room. When they did finally arrive, they were somewhat compressed and distressed!

Left: Iris Weber, the future Mrs Phillips. Right: Torquay, 1949. The couple's honeymoon was blessed with ten days of sunshine.

Torquay was blessed with 10 days of glorious sunshine and warm weather, and during our stay I decided to take a risk and teach Iris to drive! She was an excellent pupil, and when the honeymoon was over she drove us home via Bournemouth, to lunch with my parents, before heading for our new flat in St John's Wood. Alas my finances did not stretch to running a flat, a car and a wife, and so reluctantly we had to part with the car. It was thus a full year before Iris could actually take her formal driving test which, of course, she passed first time.

Our first daughter, Pamela, was born in June 1951, taking us into a whole new world. Our flat only had two bedrooms, and so now one of those was for the baby. A slight snag was its proximity to the front door and hall, which also served as our dining room. It meant that every dinner party was joined by the new arrival, awoken by the sounds of voices from our guests.

Iris, who had been working at ICI, did not go back to work until after all three of our children were launched. The baby seemed to take up so much of our time that I was obliged to resign from the tennis club, and though invited to play as a visitor any time, I never found the time to accept.

A happy family: Iris with their three daughters: baby Clare, Judy and Pamela aged c. one, four and eight years respectively.

With Iris pregnant again, we were obliged us to find larger living quarters. On one outing to look at a new house in Hatch End, the agent was just locking up after us and we were getting into the car when he said, "I'm sure you had a baby when we started…." Sure enough, we did, and we had left her inside the house, still fast asleep in her carry cot! Much laughter followed. Ultimately, we found a pleasant, three-bedroom semi in Wembley Park, and our second daughter, Judy, was born in May 1954. By now we were rather more expert with babies, and Judy proved much easier to manage than her sibling.

Our innings was not yet declared, Iris announcing that she wanted another child. I assumed she wanted a boy, but was told that the sex was unimportant, she just wanted three! My initial reaction was that we couldn't afford it, but it was clear that I had little say in the matter. So in September 1958, Clare arrived and hugely added to the joy we derived from Pam and Judy.

We enjoyed a comfortable and happy life, seeing our children grow up and progress through school (all three followed their mother into South Hampstead High School) and into successful careers. Pam studied for an HND in Maths and Computing, and became something of an expert in the computing world; Judy went into teaching as Head of Languages at a secondary school; and Clare progressed to Trinity Hall, Cambridge, and similarly taught at a number of independent schools throughout the country. She is an acknowledged specialist in 17th Century literature and culture.

Summer holidays were packed with fond memories of a particular hotel we frequented on the west cliff of Bournemouth, run by a former shipping company executive and his wife who had children of similar ages to our own.

Later we ventured abroad to Austria, enjoying fabulous forest walks and wonderful mountain scenery.

With retirement came more time to invest in leisure and learning new crafts, including art and bridge. Iris became actively involved with an old people's luncheon club and was soon conscripted onto the committee. Her prior business experience coupled with her talent for figures served her well, and although I did not join the club, I was regularly roped in as a 'chauffeur'.

We moved from Wembley Park to a delightful flat in Eastcote at Georgian Lodge, moving into a ground floor apartment in 2001 in recognition of our advancing ages. The block was owned by an elderly couple in North London and managed by various agents over the years of varying degrees of skill and professionalism. One story illustrates the point.

The residents had a few minor grievances that we agreed we would discuss with the agents, a company called Warners, when we were next in North Harrow. Popping round to see them, you can imagine our surprise when we turned up at their offices to find the blinds drawn, the shutters down, and a pile of unopened post accumulating by the letter box. It was immediately clear that the proprietors had departed, and the business collapsed.

Having considered the implications of this rather startling development, we concluded that our most urgent action was to ensure that the block was still insured, since we had recently paid the agents a premium for that purpose. On the way home, we called on the brokers with whom the policy was held and were relieved to receive a sympathetic response and assurance that, although they had not received the money from Warners, the block would still be insured while we sorted things out with the landlord. From then onwards, we took a leading role in working with the landlord and a newly-appointed agent to ensure the block ran smoothly and the residents' views were recognised.

In 2010, Iris began exhibiting symptoms of acute anxiety that needed medication to control. It co-incided with my need for a hip replacement, for the purposes of which, we agreed to book ourselves into a care home. It meant that I could be sure that Iris was being looked after while I was incapacitated, and that help was on hand if she needed it. Of course, matters didn't quite work out as planned, and my scheduled operation was postponed for several months until February 2011. What was thus intended as a short stay in the care home,

131

transpired into something rather more permanent and we became progressively institutionalised.

While I was convalescing, Iris had a number of tests and scans, and the results were reassuring. Although her condition was stabilised, and my mobility was returning, we decided to stay in the home. Events, sadly, moved rapidly and conclusively.

On Monday 21 November, I had arranged to go to the Harrow Friendship Club for lunch. Iris had a cough, which was new and persistent, and I mentioned it to the nurse on duty. It was agreed that I would still go to my lunch while the nurse pursued a diagnosis. I was finishing lunch at the club when I received a message to return to the home as quickly as possible as her condition had deteriorated and the doctor did not expect her to survive another 24 hours. She died during the night of 22/23 November, and her funeral followed two days later. It was attended by a surprising number of family and friends, and paradoxically I felt that Iris would have enjoyed it. We'd been together 62 years without any major disputes and shared countless joys. The key factors contributing to this were our shared values and opinions. Surprisingly, we discovered this compatibility when we first met. Iris possessed a unique ability to put people at their ease.

The weeks following her passing were tough, but gradually I developed an ability to think about her without overbearing sadness.

My long-suffering NHS doctor, John Brewerton, once said to me in mild reproach, "You know, Humphrey, what you really need is a doctor in the cupboard." At the care home, I have the nearest equivalent. There is a qualified SRN available 24/7, plus a weekly visit for a GP with many years' geriatric experience. We are a community of 60 or so people from many walks of life and a wide range of experiences before retirement.

One of my fellow inmates, Johnny Johnstone, had, like me, served in the RAF in the second world war (he'd been a Brat), and we often spoke of our experiences. (He'd also had a hand in inventing the self-sealing valve in the air brakes in commercial vehicles.) One day, quite out of the blue, he asked me whether I'd like a trip in a helicopter. He said that he was arranging for two of his relatives to go on a sight-seeing trip and there were three seats; would I fill the third?

On the appointed day, we rendezvoused at Denham, a small airfield near Uxbridge, and I found myself promoted to the front seat, sitting alongside the pilot[92]. It was a splendid view, far superior to the one I enjoyed during my many flights in a Lancaster or Halifax.

Our flight, lasting about an hour, took us from Battersea Bridge to Tower Bridge, following the line of the Thames. Visibility was good and we flew at around 1,200 feet, thus giving us a splendid view of all the landmarks, especially the new buildings. It was an unexpected thrill for me, and all due to Johnny's extreme kindness and the hard work of his son, Stewart, in getting me to and from the aerodrome.

Life in the care home is one of routine: they have various activities throughout the week including wheelchair exercises, scrabble, crosswords and other such games, quizzes and discussion groups. We are also entertained by professionals of variable quality! It is an improvement on other homes that I hear about where residents are herded into a room to watch television, and the majority fall fast asleep until it's time for their next meal!

We are also visited by young students on work experience, an activity I thoroughly applaud. Having been involved in discussions with some of the youngsters personally, I believe we all gain from the experience.

Our food is above average and the chef tries hard to please us. There are regular meetings to review or change menus, but I suspect that money has a part to play in what we are given. My late wife's calorie-oriented rules are frequently broken as my monthly weigh-in registers yet another increase! Occasionally the chef is wont to experiment, leaving many of us baffled, and a handful reaching for the Gaviscon. One incident will amuse: one lunchtime, my fellow diners and I agreed that the soup was better than usual, and had considerably more 'body'. A moment or so later when the main course arrived, the staff apologised that there was no gravy to go with it. Apparently, we'd just eaten it!

The staff themselves come from many backgrounds and nationalities, and while humour is an essential commodity, it often loses much in translation. Looking after the elderly is doubtless a stressful and sometimes very difficult

---

[92] *Denham can trace its flying heritage back to the first world war, and was a flying training school from 1915. In the second world war, many of the glider pilots destined for Arnhem were trained at Denham.*

task, and the majority of our carers and nurses do a sterling job. Many of them go the extra mile to ensure we are well looked after.

From our side, the guests are organised into a Residents' Committee, sponsored by the management. For some reason unknown to me, I am the Chairman, and we have representatives from all three floors and an equal number of men and women. Terms of reference are vague, but we aim to deal with residents' concerns regarding the general running of the home with an emphasis on health and safety, food, and activities. Meeting six-weekly, we keep things fairly low key, but I believe we serve a useful purpose as a channel to express concerns which can also be voiced anonymously.

Notwithstanding the flaws, and a somewhat overburdened management team, I like it here. No care home can ever be equal to your own home but I am comfortable and well looked after.

Humphrey's medals including his DFC (left) and the oak leaf on his 1939-45 War Medal (right) denoting having been Mentioned in Despatches.

Chapter Ten – Final Approach

When I first thought of writing down my memories of the war and the tiny part I played in it, I thought about calling it 'Against the Odds'. It seemed to sum up how I'd survived when so many others didn't make it. A staggering number of Bomber Command aircrew lost their lives, the figure is already well known, and a great many others' lives were blighted by their experiences and the loss of close friends and family.

When I volunteered for aircrew, and remember that we were all volunteers, the war had not yet got into its stride. My best friend, John Goldhill, had joined the Territorials at the time of Chamberlain's return waving his now infamous piece of paper that promised peace in our time but in the end delivered one of the worst conflicts the world has ever seen. John was 'called up' quite soon after 3 September, and I knew then that my turn would probably come sooner rather than later. My only conscious recollection is that I did not fancy the army much, as I could not see me leaping over an assault course or thrusting a bayonet into a straw dummy, let alone the real thing.

Ultimately, I was 'bounced' into the war perhaps a little earlier than planned because my landlady, Mrs Wright, wanted her room back. Had that not happened when it did I would not have found myself in the recruiting office, wanting to join the Royal Navy and being rejected on grounds of poor health. The Royal Air Force, however, was not quite so discerning, and therefore it was by chance that I found myself part of the Junior Service.

I was quite clear that I wanted to do whatever was appropriate or necessary to stop Hitler and his evil regime. Part of my motivation, of course, stemmed from his treatment and hatred of the Jews, and his avowed intent to exterminate the entire race. I was quite clear at the time, and remain clear in my mind today, that it was not just Hitler that we were fighting, but the entire German nation and all of its people. I did not discriminate between who might have belonged to the Nazi party, and who did not.

To me, and to my way of thinking, they were all the enemy, and all had to be defeated. Hitler had come to power because of their will, and their votes. Yes, it later became an appalling example of a breakdown in honest and lawful government, but as they ruled him in, it was equally up to them to rule him out. It was essentially why I had no qualms about dropping bombs on German cities that might (and certainly did) kill German civilians. Doubtless there were the innocents among them, but, as Air Marshal Sir John Curtis KCB wrote many years later: 'If you start a major world war you expect to get a bloody nose'. It is always unfortunate when people get killed, particularly children, but we did what was absolutely necessary and our actions had a positive outcome in shortening the length of the war. Despite Goebbels, the Nazi propaganda minister, accusing us of being '*Terror Fliegers*' and 'Gangsters', we were not criminals then, and are not criminals now.

Which leads me to the point of recognition; recognition for our contribution to winning the war; and recognition for the thousands who made the ultimate sacrifice. There is no doubt that the RAF should have received equal credit for the defeat of Germany as our counterparts in the RN and the army, and any campaign medals and bars duly awarded. As with the Bomber Command 'clasp', the Bomber Command Memorial in Green Park is a welcome (and appropriate) act of remembrance, but came decades too late for the families (and especially the mothers) of sons who lost their lives. Indeed, the treatment of the men and women of Bomber Command has been little short of a disgrace, and the blame sits squarely at the feet of Winston Churchill. It was in his gift to see that the Bomber boys were rewarded, and he chose not to through political expediency and a desire to win the post-war election. As it happens, he lost.

I was largely apathetic on the subject of awards, but that's not to say that I wasn't proud of my DFC. I only find it awkward if I am asked what I got it for, or why another member of the crew (i.e. Paddy) was not recognised in the same way. I don't have an answer for them. What gave me even greater pleasure, however, were my two Mentioned in Despatches. If anything, these were more significant than my DFC. They reflected what I think was a greater contribution to the war effort than my tour of operations. I'd like to hope that some of my teaching helped a flight engineer or two in their hour of need, and perhaps even saved their lives. I'll never know.

So what was more dangerous? Operations? Or Training? The obvious answer would be to say 'operations' because every time you took off, someone was actively trying to bring you down. We also conducted a tour of operations at the height of the Battle of Berlin, when our loss ratios went through the roof.

In his book The Berlin Raids, Martin Middlebrook states that 626 Squadron sent 186 Lancasters on 16 Berlin raids for the loss of eight aircraft missing and one crashed. Fifty-six men were killed and a further nine made prisoners of war. Our colleagues at Wickenby on 12 Squadron suffered more: 78 men killed, 44 prisoners of war and five who evaded capture. Others fared even worse: 101 Squadron, the Special Duties Squadron that flew with an eighth, German-speaking radio operator to intercept and jam nightfighter transmissions, lost 133 men killed and 42 prisoners of war. What is perhaps more revealing is the loss rate as a percentage of operations flown: ours was 4.3 percent; 12 Squadron was 6.25 percent; and 101 Squadron 6.1 percent. Our Group loss rate stood at 5.5 percent, so you could say our Squadron was comparatively fortunate.

Happily, we all came through our tour in one piece, a combination of luck, expertise, and more luck. We were certainly good at our jobs, and I'd like to think that our experience helped get us through or avoid some potentially sticky situations. But there were many crews more experienced than us that never made it home, and from whom nothing was heard after take-off. Berlin proved to be the graveyard of many an exceptional pilot and crew.

Training, too, had its fair share of dangers. Many thousands of aircrew were killed before ever firing a shot or dropping a bomb in anger, and they were often killed with an experienced instructor on board. Of course, no-one is shooting at you, and so the danger comes from within, but the death toll of those in training is sufficient to illustrate that instructing was far from a 'safe' occupation. It is not surprising that many of the characters I came across could not wait to get back to the comparative 'safety' of operations, where they felt more in charge of their own destiny.

For many years after the war, I was not bothered by reunions or meeting up with my former crew. I relented when a close cousin of my wife (he had been an armourer at Wickenby after the war) made me a member of the Wickenby Register, and I started to take a more active interest. I went to a reunion and then after became something of a 'regular'. I remember one visit in particular where they had a number of photographs and documents out on display. I was taking a close look at them when this man approached me and asked me if I was Humphrey Phillips. When I confirmed who I was he sniffed: "You were a right bastard!" It transpired that he had taken over as Flight Engineer Leader after I was tour-expired, and left him with the engineers' logs to complete. He really was most put out by it, even decades after the event!

I was annoyed when alerted to a piece by the author Mel Rolfe in one of his books recounting the incident when we'd been hit by incendiaries. In fairness to Mr Rolfe, it was a simple re-telling of the story told in Eric Simms' book, Birds of the Air. It rankled me that the story was being repeated, with all of its inaccuracies and determined that I would have it out with Eric. Through the

137

auspices of his daughter, we arranged to meet, but when I did so I decided to keep my counsel. By then, the 'bird man' was quite an elderly gentleman, whose party trick was to teach a Robin to eat out of his hand. I saw nothing to be gained by causing an argument, and put it to bed, once and for all.

It was partly pique that he had taken my role in the story, and I strong objected to the exaggeration regarding how badly the mid upper had been injured. It was a difficult and dangerous situation that we'd faced, and as such I felt it did not need any further hyperbole. The action that probably saved Dick Tredwin's life was the decision to lose height because he had no oxygen. While I would concede that the aircraft was badly damaged, it is not true to say that the wings were about to fall off. And while I would also say that there was nowhere near as much blood coming from the gunner's wound as Eric implied, it is also true that Dick was unconscious for the better part of two days. I was told later that after he woke up, he honestly thought he was in a German hospital!

If I have any regrets, it is in not keeping in touch with Johnny Neilson, and my Australian friends after we parted company. 'Bluey' Graham added a DFC for a tour of operations with 550 Squadron, adding a DFC to the AFC he'd won earlier. He was discharged from the RAF in 1946 and returned to Australia. 'Shorty' was commissioned and in November 1943 converted to flying Mosquitoes. Posted to 627 Squadron, he was killed in action on 6 January, 1944, his aircraft coming to grief only a few minutes after taking off to attack Berlin. I never knew this at the time and was only made aware he had died while researching my own story.

Bluey and Shorty were my mentors. They took me under their wing and looked after me both in the air and on the ground. Although I had never had any great urge to fly, they taught me the basics, so that in an emergency I'd be able to get the aircraft back to base and give everyone a chance of baling out. I spent many hours in the Link trainer (a primitive flight simulator) and in the air, practicing a rate one turn (that is to say a 15-degree port turn). Air tests could be monotonous and dull, and the boys would liven things up by flying low through a particular valley and beating up a certain farm. I was convinced that one day we would be reported, but somehow we never were[93].

I did once have a chance meeting with Willie Caldow while I was in London on business for the 600 Group. I was in the Strand Palace Hotel, waiting by the lift door, when who should walk out but Willie with his wife and children

[93] *According to his records, 'Bluey' Graham flew a first tour of 27 operations between April and August 1942, and a second tour of 20 operations between December 1943 and May 1944.*

in tow, all looking rather glum. I was delighted to see him and said so. Unfortunately, I was running late, and said that I'd give him a ring. He seemed less than enthusiastic, but nonetheless I called a few days later, with a view to meeting up and chatting about old times. He clearly didn't want to know me, wasn't interested in a drink, and no sooner had the phone call started than it ended with him saying 'goodbye'. During the war, long after Willie had returned to operations, I had gone to see him in Scotland for the weekend, but there was a mix up over my mess bill. It would seem daft that Willie would still bear a grudge for such a minor misdemeanour, but it is the only incident I can recall where I might have blotted my copybook. It was a pity, for I'd have liked to have stayed friends. He had, after all, saved my life.

And so to return to my initial theme, I survived, against the odds. That I did so is largely down to good fortune, both in the skippers I flew with and the training we received. But more than anything, it was down to luck. Many better than me didn't make it. I will be eternally grateful that I did.

Humphrey relaxing in more recent times.

Appendix 1: The Thousand Bomber Raid Crew

Marston Moor, home to 1652 Conversion Unit, put up 12 aircraft for the raid on Cologne. In the days before Harris finally gave the order to attack, officers and men of various aircrew categories had been arriving at the unit to form into irregular ('scratch') crews, flying a handful of short air tests to familiarise themselves with their aircraft and each other. Orders had been received from 4 Group on the 22 May, informing 1652 to suspend conversion training and to make all aircraft operationally serviceable within 48 hours. Maintenance and ground crew personnel worked tirelessly to ensure the Group's orders were fulfilled. For five nights, they waited for the order to go, until finally, on the early evening of 30 May, the waiting was over. The unit's contribution was led by none other than Squadron Leader Leonard Cheshire DSO, DFC, arguably one of the most famous bomber barons of all time. He was later awarded the Victoria Cross for sustained air operations, rather than for a single feat, and survived the war.

Thirteen crews were in fact readied for operations, but on the night of the attack, one of their number failed to take off owing to mechanical trouble. Included in the 12 that finally made it into the air was the crew of Harry Drummond DFM. He had arrived on 25th with Pilot Officer Ken Allport from RAF Station Dalton. His crew comprised:

Pilot	Pilot Officer Harry Drummond DFM
Nav	Pilot Officer Ken Allport
w/op	Sergeant Frederick Simkins
FE	Sergeant Humphrey Phillips
AG	Sergeant Frederick (Eric) Hay
AG	Flight Sergeant Libere Boucher

Humphrey Phillips was the least most experienced of all of the crew, at least in terms of operational experience. He was right to be impressed by his peer's credentials, since they were all seasoned veterans.

Pilot Officer Harry Drummond had volunteered for aircrew and enlisted on 18 September, 1939, just two weeks after war was declared. Awarded his 'wings' almost exactly a year later, and promoted Sergeant, Harry was posted to 78 Squadron, Bomber Command, flying as second pilot in an Armstrong Whitworth Whitley V. Having completed his apprenticeship in the right-hand seat, he was promoted captain of his own aircraft after five operations and went on to complete another 12 before being posted to 76 Squadron to convert to four engines. A further 11 operations followed, including the now-famous attack on the Scharnhorst at La Pallice on 24 July, 1941 for which he was awarded the Distinguished Flying Medal. (Interestingly, in the recommendation for his award, the AOC 4 Group, Air Vice Marshal Roddy Carr, states '…this NCO was recommended for the DFM in a previous list…' The DFM was a comparatively rare award, at least compared to the officers' DFC.)

By the time he was 'screened', he'd completed 28 operations (17 Whitley, 11 Halifax) and was commissioned in the field. A long period of instructing followed, for which he was Mentioned in Despatches and awarded the Air Force Cross (AFC) in the New Years' Honours of 1944. Promoted Wing Commander, he assumed command of 1658 HCU, and with the end of the war in sight, was posted to Italy to become Wing Commander, heavy bomber operations. The raids on Cologne and Essen were his 29th and 30th bomber operations respectively, and his total for the war stood at 34 to 21 different targets.

Donald Kenneth (Ken) Allport had a long and distinguished career in the RAF. Having joined the RAFVR and flown operations with 10 Squadron in the winter of 1940/1941, he converted to the Halifax with 102 Squadron at Topcliffe before being posted to 158 Squadron. Recognised for his skills as a navigator, and commissioned, he rose quickly through the ranks before being singled out to join the elite Pathfinder Force (PFF). Spells with 35 Squadron and 97 Squadron saw him fly with several senior officers, including Group Captain Noel 'Press-on' Fresson and Wing Commander Eric Carter, both well-known PFF 'personalities'.

He was awarded a DFC in May 1943, the first of three gallantry awards. A Distinguished Service Order followed in November, the citation reading: "As navigator, this officer has participated in a large number of sorties, many of them demanding a high degree of skill and determination. Nevertheless, Squadron Leader Allport has executed his tasks with exceptional ability and his faultless work has contributed in a large measure to the successes obtain. His achievements are worthy of the highest praise."

By the end of the war. Ken had notched up more than 60 operations and added a Bar to his DFC. Posted to Transport Command, he flew with 511 and 242 Squadrons, navigating a variety of different aircraft. Appointed to a permanent commission, after spells with Flying Training Command, Ken re-joined Bomber Command on V-Force, flying the Vickers Valiant. During the Suez conflict, he bombed targets in Egypt, and later served with the USAF on intelligence duties. He retired from the RAF as a wing commander on 13th April 1972. Wing Commander Ken Allport DSO DFC* RAF died peacefully in McLaren Vale, Australia, in 2011, aged 93.

Sergeant Frederick Henry George Simkins was born in Wandsworth and enlisted at RAF Uxbridge in Middlesex. After the usual training to become a Wireless Operator/Air Gunner, he was posted to 104 Squadron at Driffield, flying a number of operations to attack German port and harbour installations as well as enemy warships in the winter of 1941/42. Posted to 158 Squadron at Driffield, he continued to fly operations to a number of heavily-defended targets, including Essen and Duisberg in the Ruhr. Many of these operations were flown with his 'regular' skipper, Sergeant Dennis Webb (later DFC, MiD), as well as two of 158 Squadron's more senior officers, Squadron Leader Anthony Ennis DSO, DFC and Squadron Leader Francis Hewitt OBE. Sergeant Frederick Simkins was killed in action on 20 July 1942 while air bomber in the crew of Pilot Officer Horace Skelly. He was 32, and left a widow, Miriam Rosalie Tomkins, whom he'd married in 1935. Frederick has no known grave and is commemorated on the Runnymede Memorial. He is also remembered on the Roll of Honour, a WW2 memorial stone inside the Soldiers' Chapel at the parish church of St. James the Great at Hanslope, in the Milton Keynes area of Buckinghamshire.

Sergeant Frederick 'Eric' Hay was a Geordie, born on 20 May 1920 in Newcastle Upon Tyne. A librarian before the war, he joined the RAF Volunteer Reserve and qualified as a Wireless Operator/Air Gunner. His qualities took him to 35 Squadron PFF operating from Graveley, where he flew a number of operations – usually as a 'Backer-up' – against heavily defended targets, including Berlin, Hamburg and Wilhelmshafen. He also went to Lorient to attack the U-Boat pens on at least three occasions. Sadly, within a year of the Thousand Bomber Raids he was dead, killed in action 14 April 1943, when his Halifax was intercepted and shot down by a German nightfighter from a height of c18,000ft during an attack on Stuttgart. Eric died alongside his skipper, Pilot Officer Ron Wilkes DFM, and two other members of the crew. Eric had married in July 1941, and his son, Michael Ronald Hay, was born three months after his death, his names derived from Frederick's 35 Squadron skipper and a fellow air gunner.

Flight Sergeant Libere Joseph Boucher was a member of the Royal Canadian Air Force who later went on to win a DFM in December 1942 while serving with 405 (RCAF) Squadron. The citation, published in an edition of Flight magazine, reads simply: 'As wireless operator/air gunner, this airman has participated in many attacks on the enemy's industrial centres in the Ruhr, as well as important ports such as Hamburg, Brest, St. Nazaire and Kiel.'

ORDER OF BATTLE - COLOGNE

Those operating on the night of 30/31 May from 1652 (as listed in order in the ORB) were as follows:

Squadron Leader Leonard Cheshire DSO, DFC and crew
Flight Lieutenant Robert Norman and crew
Flight Lieutenant Peter Johnston DFC and crew
Flight Lieutenant Stanley Wright and crew
Flying Officer Keith Cresswell and crew
Flying Officer Kenneth Whisken and crew
Flying Officer John Trethewy and crew
Pilot Officer Robert Langton DFM and crew
Pilot Officer Harry Williams and crew
Pilot Officer Leonard Whyte and crew
Flight Sergeant George Herbert and crew
Flight Sergeant Eric Borsberry and crew
Pilot Officer Harry Drummond and crew

Of events that night: Robert Norman returned early with engine trouble; Johnston suffered a hang up as did Leonard Whyte; Trethewy returned early having identified the wrong target; Eric Borsberry failed to take off; Wright failed to return.

Included in the crew of Peter Johnston was Thomas Sankey DFM, who had served with Humphrey at 460 Conversion Flight. Included in the crew of Robert Norman was Pilot Officer Reginald Petherbridge, an experienced air gunner who was shortly after killed with 158 Squadron.

Robert Norman went on to win the DFC and was later Mentioned in Despatches as a wing commander.

Peter Johnston had won his DFC in 1941 with 35 Squadron, and was Mentioned in Despatches for his time as an instructor at 1652, being directly credited with supplying 4 Group with 27 trained captains. He was later killed in action almost exactly a year later (30 May 1943) on an operation to Wuppertal.

Keith Cresswell, an old boy of Imperial Service College, won the DFC in 1942 and added a DSO the following year for operations against targets in the Ruhr and Italy. He added a bar to his DSO in 1944.

Ken Whisken was awarded the DFC in March 1942 with 102 Squadron. He was killed in air operations while still with 1652 CU on 26 June 1942. He was 23.

John Trethewy was killed while still serving with 1652 CU on 17 August, 1942.

Robert Langton, a former Halton Apprentice (22nd Entry), won his DFM for a tour with 102 Squadron flying Whitleys in the winter of 1940/1941, and was commissioned in the summer of '41. Langton was a long-time servant of the instructing world, becoming Chief Flying Instructor of 1666 HCU in the acting rank of wing commander, winning the AFC. He was killed in action at the age of 30 on operations to Walcheren with 76 Squadron.

Harry Williams was awarded the DFM in March 1942 for his time as a sergeant pilot with 35 Squadron for 'gallantry and devotion to duty in the execution to air operations'.

Leonard Whyte was awarded the DFC with 10 Squadron in August 1942, shortly after taking part in the Thousand Bomber Raids. He received a Bar to his DFC as an acting wing commander with 102 Squadron, and survived the war.

George Herbert won the DFM while serving with 76 Squadron and later went on to PFF. Unusually, for a former Public Schoolboy, he served first as a sergeant pilot before being commissioned. He was killed in action with 35 Squadron over Munster in 12 June, 1943. A memorial to George and his crew was unveiled in Holland in 2015.

Eric Borsberry went on to win the DFM in August 1942 with 76 Squadron. He was later commissioned.

Appendix 2: Order of Battle - Essen

Those operating on the night of 1/2 June from 1652 (as listed in order in the ORB) were as follows:

Squadron Leader Leonard Cheshire DSO, DFC and crew
Flight Lieutenant Robert Norman and crew
Flight Lieutenant Peter Johnston DFC and crew
Flying Officer Keith Cresswell and crew
Flying Officer Kenneth Whisken and crew
Flying Officer John Trethewy and crew
Pilot Officer Robert Langton DFM and crew
Pilot Officer Harry Williams and crew
Pilot Officer Leonard Whyte and crew
Flight Sergeant George Herbert and crew
Flight Sergeant Eric Borsberry and crew
Pilot Officer Harry Drummond and crew

In this raid, three 1,000-pounders refused to release from the Halifax of John Trethewy and later had to be jettisoned. He also suffered electrical failures, rendering his turrets u/s. Whyte also suffered a hang up, while Herbert lost an engine. Harry Williams failed to return, but survived as a prisoner of war.

Accompanying Cheshire was the station commander, Group Captain John Bradbury DFC. Bradbury was a veteran of the Royal Flying Corps, and an active service pilot in the inter-war years being awarded his DFC in 1934. He was Officer Commanding 77 Squadron at the start of the war, and appointed station commander at Marston Moor in October 1941. He retired from the RAF in 1949.

Appendix 3: 626 Squadron Losses between 22 November 1943 and 18 July 1944

1943	Pilot	Casualties
26/27 November	Flight Sergeant Windus	7 KIA
	Flight Sergeant C J E Kindt	7 KIA
	Flight Lieutenant V Wood	All safe
2/3 December	Squadron Leader George Roden DFC	7 KIA; 1 PoW

1944		
2/1 January	Sergeant Ernest Berry	6 KIA; 1 PoW
14/15 January	Flight Sergeant Kenneth Elkington	7 KIA
	Flight Sergeant Norman West	7 KIA
27/28 January	Flight Lieutenant William Belford	6 KIA; 1 PoW
30/31 January	Flying Officer John Wilkinson	7 KIA
15/16 February	Flight Sergeant J Jacques	1 KIA; 6 POW
19/20 February	Flight Sergeant Alexander Matheson	7 KIA
24/25 February	Flying Officer J Hutchinson DFC	8 KIA
22/23 March	Flying Officer G D Kewley	7 KIA
24/25 March	Wing Commander Q Ross	7 KIA
	Flight Sergeant Keith Margetts	7 KIA
24/25 April	Warrant Officer M McPherson	7 KIA
	Warrant Officer V H Bernyk	7 KIA
	Flight Sergeant F B Baker	7 KIA
3/4 May	Flight Sergeant P J Barkway	7 KIA
	Pilot Officer D S Jackson DFC	7 KIA
	Pilot Officer N J Fisher	7 KIA

11/12 May	Pilot Officer C R Marriott DFM	7 KIA
21/22 May	Pilot Officer R R Brant	6 KIA, 1 evaded
27/28 May	Pilot Officer R F Ayres	5 KIA; 1 POW; 1 evaded
22/23 June	Sergeant R A Woolley	7 KIA
30 June/1 July	Pilot Officer W F Pocock	7 KIA
	Pilot Officer A Orr	4 KIA; 2 PoW; 1 evaded
7 July	Pilot Officer J C Oram	2 KIA

Appendix 4: Aircraft flown in by F/L Humphrey Phillips DFC and their fates.

Halifax

R9379 Stalled on approach to Elsham Wolds and spun into fields Aug 42
R9380 Tyre burst on T/O from Lindholme, swung; u/c collapsed Aug 43
R9390 SOC Feb 45
R9422 SOC Nov 43
R9423 Undercarriage collapsed on landing at Marston Moor Jul 43
R9426 Swung on heavy landing at Pocklington and u/c collapsed Mar 43
R9429 Swung on take-off at Riccall and hit gun emplacement Dec 43
R9432 (Both 1,000 bomber raids.) Converted to 3956M Jul 43
R9523 Converted to 3690M May 43
R9532 FTR Jun 42 with 102 Sqn
R9565 Swung on heavy landing at Pocklington and u/c collapsed Nov 42
V9882 35 Sqn and 102 Conversion Flight. Crashed and burned May 42.
V9983 Crashed near Haxey, Lincs, after take-off from Blyton Feb44
V9987 FTR from Bremen Jun 42
W1004 SOC Jan44
W1011 Crash landed and caught fire on approach to landing Dec 42
W1216 FTR from Aachen with 103 Sqn Oct 42
W1220 FTR from Bremen with 103 Sqn Oct 42
W4851
W7819 SOC Nov 45 after service with 103CF and 1656.
W7846 Served with 103 Sqn, 1656 and 1662. Ended in a ditch at Blyton, Mar 44
DG 219 Crashed in circuit at Broadway Stanworth, near Lindholme, May 44
DG 484 Halifax II.
BB264 U/c and tail wheel ripped off landing at Lindholme Apr 44

Manchester

L7460 Flew with 97, 83, 50 and 57 Sqns prior to 1656 CU. SOC Jul 43.
L7479 Flew with 25 OTU then 48 Sqn. FTR on first Thousand Bomber Raid.
L7626
R5780 8, 106, 49 and 57 Sqns then 1656 CU. Crashed Lichfield, Oct 42.

Lancaster

ED324   Served in training units throughout. Became 5290M
ED381   Collided with a Wellington over Brize Norton in Jun 43
ED383   Crashed at Lakenheath in Feb with a remarkable 628 hours.
ED567   With 1 LFS. Crashed May 44.
ED585   Lancaster III. Later flew with 50 Sqn and SOC in Apr 45.
ED607   Served in training units throughout. Finally SOC in 47.
W4263   Later flew with 460 and 625 Sqns. SOC Jan47.
W4264   Became 5289M
W4328   Flew with 103 and 12 Sqns before joining 1656. SOC Jan 47.
W4374   Crashed in a wood at Apley in Jun 43.
W4521
W4776   SOC after its third crash, Oct 43, having flown 495 hours
W4779   Became 4903M
W4780   Flown later by 166 Sqn; shot down over Berlin, Jan 44 after 34 hours.
W4781   Crashed in Aug 43 having flown 329 hours
W4793   F- Freddie. 12 Sqn and 1LFS; crashed in May 44 with 616 hours.
W4821   103 Sqn and 300 Sqn, 1656, 1LFS and 6LFS. SOC Mar 47.
W4824   467 and 50 Sqns. FTR from daylight raid in Aug 44 with 619 hours.
W4834   Flown by 57 Sqn after 1656. Blown up at Scampton in Mar 43.
W4845   Became 5291M after serving with 1LFS
W4851   1656 after 156 Sqn. Burned in a crash Jun 44 with 744 hours.
W4854   M – Mother. 156 Sqn; shot down over Pilsen, Apr 43.
W4857   With 103 Sqn. Crashed approaching Elsham Wolds, Feb 43.
W4883   Q – Queenie. Involved in three separate crashes and later served
        with 231 Sqn. SOC in Dec 46.
W4885   1662CU, 622 Sqn, 5LFS, 90 Sqn, and 10MU. SOC Jan 47.
W4890   Exclusively training units Crashed at Thorney Island in Feb 45.
W4965   Conversion and training units. Crashed May 44, with 566 hours.
W4980   1656CU, 155 Sqn, 3LFS, 90 Sqn, and 1662CU. SOC in Jul 45.
W5009   101 and 625 Sqns. FTR Nuremberg Mar 44, with 458 hours.
R5491   61 Sqn prior to service with 1656CU. Wrecked in May 43.
R5500   Served with 207 and 460 Sqns prior to 1656CU. Became 4902M.
R5507   Z-Zebra with 207 Sqn. Also 101 Sqn and 1 LFS. Recorded as J –
        Johnnie whilst at 1656. SOC Nov 45.
R5672   83 Sqn prior to 1656CU. Flew 341 hours before crashing in Aug 43.
R5677   106 Sqn (as B-Baker), FTR May 43 after 67 ops and 512 hours.
LM305   1656; missing on exercise flight with 210 hours in May 43.
JB599   Q-2 626 Sqn (every trip to Berlin was in this a/c). Ultimately went
        missing in Mar 44 with Pilot Officer Kewley at the controls.

Appendix 5: The Flight Engineers' Exam

Hydraulics

1. Describe all methods by which the undercarriage will lower.

2. Describe your action on Pilot's report that:

   a. undercarriage fails to lower
   b. wing flaps fail to lower
   c. bomb doors fail to open

3. In the case of 2(a) above, would you retract undercarriage again? If not, give reason. IN the case of 2(c) above, would you close bomb doors again? If not, give reason.

4. State pressures in the following accumulators indicating position of service at stated pressure:

   a. main undercarriage
   b. undercarriage doors
   c. wing flaps
   d. Lockheed accumulator

5. Explain the purpose and give a brief description of the 'mechanised lock'. How is it possible to ascertain if the lock is engaging correctly?

6. Explain the difference between the system a. fitted with Messier pump, b. Lockheed pump.

Power Unit

1. State operational limitations of the Merlin XX

   a. coolant outlet temperature
   b. oil inlet temperature
   c. Min. oil pressures

2. What is the recommended temperature range for coolant during cruising and what is the method of maintaining this?

3. Describe the procedure for feathering a propeller. What important check should the pilot make on feathering an inboard motor?

4. Give r.p.m. and boost pressures for:

    a. Maximum economical cruising)
    b. Maximum climbing   ) State time limit
    c. Special emergency cruising   )

5. Name all auxiliaries mounted on port inner motor

6. You are flying at economic 'cruising'. What advice would you give and what conclusions would you arrive at if the pilot reports that the starboard outer engine's boost pressure has jumped to +10lbs/sq.in?

Electrical System

1. Name services supplied by S.I. generator

2. The wireless operator reports that the port outer generator is not charging.

    a. how does he know this?
    b. What action would you take?

3. How many fuses are there in the bomb circuits; what are they, and where are they situated? (Latest operational aircraft).

4. Mounted on the starboard leg of the starboard undercarriage and linked to the mud scraper is an electrical switch. What is its purpose?

Oxygen Economiser System

1. How do you test your point for correct flow?

2. You have turned the master cocks on 2/3rds of its travel and detect an escape of oxygen from the gland. What action do you take?

3. The rear gunner complains that he is receiving no oxygen. What is the first point you would check?

Fuel Systems

1. Make a sketch of the system showing tank capacities (without extended range tanks).

2. Give sequence for tank changing using number 5 and 6 tanks only.

3. You are flying on Nos 2 and 3 tanks. Describe procedures on order from captain to jettison fuel.

4. What is the minimum air pressure for jettisoning fuel?

Drills

1. State the points you would check inside the aircraft before flight.

2. State the responsibilities of the engineer in the case of:

   a. dinghy drill
   b. parachute drill

3. Tabulate procedure for loading and launching a photo-flash.

General

1. a. How do you release a 1000lb bomb manually?
   b. What is the procedure for jettisoning bombs?

2. a. If 'George' is to be used, what must be checked prior to take off?
   b. Will George function without the switch marked 'auto control' on?

3. a. What increase in fuel consumption will the use of the boost cut-out entail?
   b. What is the correct method of cruising to give most economical fuel consumption?

4. a. How many fire extinguishers are there on the Halifax?
   b. You are at the flare chute: where is the nearest extinguisher?

Sources

RAF records from The National Archive

AIR 14/2155 (1668 Flying Syllabus)
AIR 28/90
AIR 29/612
AIR 29/613
AIR 29/614
AIR 29/850
AIR 29/857

Flying log books

Logbook of Humphrey Phillips DFC
Logbook of Harry Drummond AFC, DFM

Diaries

The private diaries of H.B.Phillips

Acknowledgements by Sean Feast

My first thanks must go to Humphrey, who wrote to me in early 2016 having read *An Alien Sky*. Humphrey had an idea or two for a book on some of the unsung heroes of Bomber Command, but it fast became apparent to me that Humphrey's own story was a remarkable one worth telling. It has been a privilege to have spent the last 12 months researching his life, and looking forward to our fortnightly chats. My thanks also to his daughters, and especially Clare Wikeley, for helping move things along smoothly.

Many people have helped in bringing Humphrey's story to life, and whereas there is always the danger of missing someone out, the following deserve special mention: Ann Law at the RAF Wickenby Memorial Collection; Tom Bint of the 626 Squadron Association for information and access to squadron photographs; Peter Coulter (yet again!) of the 550 Squadron Association; The Rushden Heritage Trust for the photograph of Keith Margetts; Ian Hay for details, information and the photograph of his grandfather 'Eric' Hay; Pete Cook for copies of Harry Drummond's log book; Wing Commander Mike Allport for information and photographs about his father, Wing Commander Ken Allport; David Fell for the photograph (published for the first time) of

David Holford. The photograph of H.H.Drummond AFC, DFM is courtesy of the M.F.Chandler Collection with sincere thanks. The photograph of Wally Lashbrook comes via fellow author Graham Pitchfork.

The photographs of bomb damage from the Cooks Tour come via my good friend, Mike King.

Bibliography

A Pathfinder's War – Grub Street 2009 – Sean Feast
Birds of the Air – Hutchinson 1976 – Eric Simms
Bomber Command Losses 1943 and 1944 – Midland Counties Publications – Bill Chorley
Lancaster Target – Goodall 1977 – Jack Currie
The Berlin Raids – Viking 1988 – Martin Middlebrook
The Halifax File – Air Britain 1982
The Lancaster – Airlife 2001 (second edition) – Harry Holmes
To Strive and Not to Yield – Woodfield 2002 – Dennis West
103 Squadron Profile – Mention the War 2016 – Chris Ward

Printed in Great Britain
by Amazon